MLK
TREATISES FROM MY LIFE

ROSE CAMPBELL

MLK: TREATISES FROM MY LIFE
Copyright © 2022 **Rose Campbell**

All rights reserved. No part of this book may be used or reproduced by any means, graphic, electronic, or mechanical, including photocopying, recording, taping or by information storage and retrieval system without the written permission of the author except in the case of brief quotations embodied in critical articles and reviews.

Stratton Press Publishing
831 N Tatnall Street Suite M #188,
Wilmington, DE 19801
www.stratton-press.com
1-888-323-7009

Because of the dynamic nature of the Internet, any web addresses or links contained in this book may have changed since publication and may no longer be valid. The views expressed in the work are solely those of the author and do not necessarily reflect the views of the publisher, and the publisher hereby disclaims any responsibility for them.

Any people depicted in stock imagery provided by Shutterstock are models, and such images are being used for illustrative purposes only.

ISBN (Paperback): 978-1-64895-799-4
ISBN (Ebook): 978-1-64895-800-7

Printed in the United States of America

INTRODUCTION

MLK Treatises

Welcome. My name is Rose Campbell. My role as a psychic medium is to be a conduit of information from those who no longer have a physical body but who still have consciousness. They have consciousness not only of the realm they now inhabit but of our world, their former realm, as well.

Not all things are remembered once a being crosses the *veil* between worlds, but things of significant emotional impact and rooting are.

It is why we can remember our loved ones or happenings that may have made an indelible emotional memory.

Our passions, our disappointments, our driving urges—all of which are based in our emotional fields and are remembered as well. However, more mundane details of our lives are lost once the physical brain dies. Only the emotional energy imprints are stored in our eternal consciousness.

During the work I was doing on my first channeled book, *The Princess and the Peon: An Uncommon Conversation with the Late Princess Diana* (Stratton Press 2019), I was approached by the spirit of Martin Luther King Jr. to work with him as well. While I was both surprised and honored, I felt I had no choice but to decline his invitation. I was not only involved in writing my Diana book but working full-time and raising four children. (I still marvel at how I did all of that.) I did not want to say no, but my candle was already burning at both ends.

When he approached me again in 2006, I was freer than I had been in 1998. The children were older, the Diana book was finished, and I had no other major spiritual works that were taking all my free time. I was a bit leery of taking on a major project, but I felt truth in his words and his need to say his piece, so to speak. Thus, I signed on to be his *secretary*. His asking me to be his secretary caused me some amusement at first, I must admit, but then I realized that was exactly what my role was: I was secretary to those who no longer have a voice in our world.

Since he had approached me in 1998 to work with him as I found myself with more free time and an urge to take on another major project, I began to think about him and wondered if he had found another secretary.

I also realized I knew very little about the man, other than having a holiday named after him, that he was a civil rights leader, and his death caused some riots.

Some of you might wonder how I knew so little of him, given his prominence nowadays.

I was twelve when he died. My first introduction to him was the riots (which my mother got caught in—a funny story for another time). When I asked who he was, my uncle gave me an answer, which will not be repeated here for it is now known how politically incorrect that answer was. It did seem my uncle had no love for his work.

His story did not make the history books until long after I finished high school, and not having gone to college, I didn't study him when the history books caught up with his history.

Quite honestly, a white kid growing up in the cornfields of Indiana surrounded by white folks didn't get to hear conversations about MLK. Even when I began to work, I worked in *white-bread* areas with women who didn't talk about him. Thus, I admit I was civil rights ignorant until Martin came calling, and I did research upon him. I was impressed.

What follows in this book, the really important parts, are his words as given to me verbatim. As with my Diana book, I will use the transcripts to convey his words to me with some comments also made by me.

It was apparent to me that he really did want to correct some things from his former life and to still use his *pulpit* to admonish us to a higher and better way.

Some of his thoughts were astonishing to me, and some were so well said that I was often in awe during this time with him. He is a great orator even in death!

When Martin began to speak about his death, I was not only sad but also intrigued.

Not many had given me such accounts. When he spoke of the pool of consciousness he was taken to, I was enthralled. Again, this was an afterlife account I had never heard. When he spoke about how he used the wrong motivation for some of his work, I was floored. So much of what he said had me mesmerized.

I hope you enjoy your time in exploring Martin's words and that they help to make the impact that I know he wanted to make.

ACCEPTING ASSIGNMENTS

What follows below, before we get into the meat of Martin's treatises, is a session where I *met* MLK and another where I ascertain if he was still interested in working with me.

These sessions were eight years apart because I had been working with Diana, Princess of Wales, when first approached by Martin. Actually, Diana also popped in to say a few words, which was nice but unexpected. It had been a while since I had spoken with her.

This section is setting the stage, so to speak, for the treatises to come.

Session (December 1, 1997)

(*While in a standard session with my own guides, after they deliver some other information to me, they make me aware that someone else wishes to speak to me.*)

GUIDES. Allow us now to work with you on giving you the connection to the one who desires your abilities and allow him to speak for himself. It is of our will that you do so, and we humbly ask that you give to us your agreement to do so. May we proceed with the connection?

ROSE. Sure, why not. I know now that I have the right to choose or deny this assignment, and I will speak to him and work on deciding my part in this as I have done with Diana. Go ahead.

ROSE CAMPBELL

G. It is our will for you to work with him as you have the others. We will make the initial contact, and when the connection is well-established, we will allow you to speak to him with great clarity. Allow us a few moments to prepare and then speak to him as if he were with you.

(*I wait a few minutes as suggested.*)

R. Hello. Are you ready to speak to me? Please be clear and give me as much information on who you are as possible.

MARTIN. I am ready and I thank you for the opportunity to speak to you. There is a great disparity between the lives of the ones who founded this nation and the ones who were brought here to help with building of the other men's dreams.

I am one who could not correlate the process of thinking that if one is of one color then they are of superior wisdom and grace within God's design for the world.

There are many who would make this a gulf of irreconcilable differences, but this is not a work that can be held up to the light of truth and be made to appear as anything other than a blockage of the light as it appears from the very heart of God.

It is an abomination that there can exist within an enlightened world the form of darkness that is expressed when there is hate and injustice for those who were also chosen to be made men in the image of God. It is a calling to the world of radical ideas that there is one set of rules for the ones chosen to be born with skin of ivory and another set of rules for everyone of another hue.

There is no difference found within the gift of God's words for the Israelites than there is found today. There is no land of milk and honey if there can be slavery for those who are his

MLK: TREATISES FROM MY LIFE

chosen ones, and all who were created in his image are chosen as his sons.

The holding of any into bondage is of a loathsome thing to the nature of God and if there be a man who can justify it with the Word of God, allow him to set an example so that I may understand.

There are many who would argue that God ordered the enslaving of the ones who were not the chosen, but this is not of any great and logical sense when applied to the words of Christ when he said that to love one another as our brothers was the newer commandment.

It is true that the Israelites took for themselves the spoils and slaves from within the encampments that they encountered, but this is not of great value either when viewed through the lens of Christian compassion and love as taught by his Son.

There can be a form of slavery where one does not own the other but does not allow the other equal freedoms. The bonds of prejudice and hate are as strong as the manacles used to bind the feet of people who were exploited into slavery.

There is no greater form of slavery than always being the one who must work or think or live where others decide that it is permissible.

I am giving you this so that you will know that I speak not only for those of a certain skin color, or even of a certain sex, but for all who are held in bondage by the small mindedness of another. There is no greater need or call to be addressed than the freedom of someone to live up to their God-given potential and to have the right to be treated as a brother or a sister. Allowing this error of thought to make its appearance within the world at any place or time does not but allow the light of God to be placed under a bushel basket of men's making.

Freedom to create and be radiant in God's image is in serious threat when another may decide for you who you are to be, where you may worship, and how you may express your God-given talents.

The freedoms that I appeal for are those to be what one will be and to have the freedom to shine forth the light of God from within without having a bushel basket of hate and prejudice blanketing the entire thought of an individual because of his or her skin color and his or her sex.

It is not enough to allow others to work where they will, it must be an entire way of life and of being for the light to shine as it is intended. Make no man a slave, and there shall be no man who is not served.

R.   Okay, but are you going to tell me your name? At least something that will dispel any doubts about your identity?

M.   I am going to work with the name that I had while there, and for your reference, I am that which was known as Martin Luther King Jr. I was a poor black farmer's son, and I grew up with the prejudice that existed in the south throughout my life. I was not allowed to go to school with the whites, and that was my earliest recalling of being treated less than the person who had another skin color.

I used to watch the white children go to school, and I knew that they had better schools and supplies, and yet they seemed not to notice the difference as much as I did. I suppose if I had been white, then I too would not have noticed the lack of things given to another.

MLK: TREATISES FROM MY LIFE

There were very poor whites who lived near us, but still they had the respect that I felt the lack of.

It was never a given that I would become the leader for civil rights that I did become. It was just something that I grew into as I read and deciphered the will of God for myself. I gave up my ministry to help the ones who were oppressed, not because there was a conflict of interest, but because there was a feeling of a new calling within my heart, and a house divided will not be built with a strong foundation.

It was to no avail to work from the pulpit to organize the freedom marches and pressures, for there was no public forum if you were concentrating on the ones who knew they were oppressed. It had to be brought to the streets and had to be made public in the political arena rather than just in the religious world.

It is a sad statement of affairs when the words of God holds no effect upon the minds of men, but that is the way I understood the issue to be.

It was with regret that I gave up my religious ministry, but it had to be a priority that I reach those who were of a nonreligious mind, for they were the greatest force behind the hate and anger. It would not have done for me to assume that a man of religion would sway those who had spurned the name of God and religion for the purpose if hate and prejudice.

I am not saying that I was unaware that many of religious persuasion were not of the guilty also. Many great atrocities have been done in the name of the Lord, and this was another reason that I felt I had to forego the way of being a man of the Lord. I had to reach out to them as a another man—nothing less, nothing more—and hope that they could see the dream and the vision that I held as being the one to make the hate and prejudice cease.

I was never in doubt that I could reach some, and I was never in doubt that I could reach many, but I was in doubt that I could bring about the reformation and restoration that I desired within the world's attitude about segregation, work equality, and access to the realm of being an American citizen with full rights and respect for those who not yet known these things.

My father once said to me that if every man could but read and every man could but work with his hands to earn his just due, then there would be no poor, and there would be no one to whom charity had to be given. I felt his words to me were prophetic within the intent, and I made it a cause to see if he was right.

I marched to Selma, not just for the civil rights of the blacks but for the rights of every individual who had the dream to forgo the tyranny of having someone stop them from being who they might become and having what they might earn.

I am well aware that I am known as the black civil rights leader, but that is not what I wish to be remembered for. I aided not only those of dark skin but also those who were the fellow members of the underprivileged and held-down societies. I began my marches with the clear idea of being the one who took the plight of the nation's prejudiced against to the streets, hoping to make the world see that there was an overwhelming amount of hate and prejudice that existed within our nation and to put a spotlight upon it.

I am grievous that the world felt me only the champion of the blacks for that was yet only another example of the way

MLK: TREATISES FROM MY LIFE

in which the world could only see in black-and-white and not the true heart of the matter at hand. While it is true that the blacks had the most boisterous voice, there was indeed a calling out by others.

There will always exist some of prejudice if we allow ourselves to only see issues as black-and-white instead of the basic needs of humans to be free to be who they were intended to be by their Creator.

If I work with you for the purpose of setting the record straight, I would wish that you give this some thought. I know that you have very little knowledge of my life for the ones who approached you with this have instructed me of this fact and want me to give you the will to work also with a knowledge of what I stood for and why I need to work with the world again to make them see that I was not only a leader for the black equality movement but for the furthering of basic human rights for all who are being oppressed.

Please make this a priority to find out what I stood for and why I led the marches. It will only help us in the formation of another attack upon the forces that would enslave the down-trodden through ignorance and lack of respect for their basic humanness.

I am going to let you get settled with this idea and allow you time to research my life, then we will speak again. It will serve us both well if you understand who I was and who I am now. It is not the one and the same, yet I cannot really say that I have changed for the better or the worst.

It is more appropriate that now I have a clarity that was not there while I lived among the trees. The forest is so much clearer now that I can have a bird's-eye view of the terrain.

This is the best analogy that I have for you. How mighty does the eye become when the scales are lifted!

Give my words some thought and reflection. I will await your approach again for the continuation of our dialogue.

Many thanks to you and your friends here for the great honor of speaking again to the world of the men who were truly created in the image of God. If the world could only conceive that thought in its totality, then my work would never have begun. May our worlds help one another to see this concept and to remove the bushel baskets that exist to further restrict the light of God and his truths.

Session (April 10, 2006)

R.   Thank you for some very powerful sessions during this last weekend. What would be your advice for even better effects, and how can we make my service to you and this world better?

G.   There is nothing wrong with your receptive powers. You are indeed a gifted and powerful voice for our world.

There are, however, issues with your ability to know when we have spoken our last in this form of communication, and with this, we will aid you. When the information is complete, there will be a closing sentence.

It will be of a formal and definitive nature to leave you no doubt that we have signed off with the relaying of information. Do not close the connection to our world until you have been given a signal such as this.

R.   Okay, got that. Is there a better format to follow?

MLK: TREATISES FROM MY LIFE

G.   Your explanation of our system to others has no need to be revamped, but you might be allowing us too little freedom in our quest to aid others of understanding their own gifts. We would suggest that you allow us to explain the concepts and offer only a few comments of your own.

R.   Okay, but your language is often so formal that it is hard for people to follow. Why is this?

G.   There are no set formats for our language as you have put it. It is your mind that has created a need for formalized distinction of your own thoughts and ours. We do not speak to you in a form of language but rather in forms of energy emanations. The language that you hear is set forth by your own center of communication, and it is with this that you communicate. If you seek to hear something more logical to others, then allow your own thoughts to be given in conjunction with our own. You do this regularly, and it would behoove you to do this more.

R.   Okay, so how?

G.   We are in your thoughts at all times. There is no distinction anymore between you and we. You have full access to our thoughts as we have of yours. Let yourself be guided by what you know to be our way of thinking. Let yourself become that which is of our energy. Do not see us as different than you but rather as an extension of each other.

R.   So are you a part of me?

G.   We are not of you, and yet we are as all things are of the One. You are a finely tuned homing device for us. We are locked into your energy as you are into ours. The gifts we give to you for others are from their sources using us as a relaying tool. There will be more of this knowledge given to you in a short time. Your work with others, be they of our world or your world, is not funneled through any but us. We are the ones who make all connections to you and others.

R.   When did this become that way?

G.   It was intended when you journeyed from our world to the world you now inhabit. It was given to you, and you accepted. From the moment of your birth upon that existence, you have been linked to our thoughts.

We were with you even as you learned to walk and talk. The way was shown to you for the recovery of that connection when you were most asking for help, and it has been strengthened in the moments of connection to each other over the years of your tuning to us. *We* have become one as was intended by the One.

R.   What is my purpose here? Is it to work with Diana, to work for the recovery of information for others as I do in sessions, or to bring through information from the Brethren? By the way, are you the Brethren?

G.   We are not the ones who have utilized you for that work known as the work of the Brethren. They are a group of ascended light energies who have come to help with technological advances upon your world. They are indeed eager to reconnect with you, and we would advise that as a means to further some work that needs accomplished upon your world. *We* are the ones who facilitate that connection for you. *We* are the ones assigned to be your gatekeepers for those who wish to enter your consciousness. *We* are your guides and the ones who work with you when you work with others.

R.   Okay, but back to my purpose.

MLK: TREATISES FROM MY LIFE

G. There is no purpose predestined for you except to be a mouth-piece for those who need voices upon your world. Of this you were informed and your consent given. You may choose to work with all who are of need for that purpose. Your role with the one known as Diana is indeed a significant one, and she wishes to interject a moment of thought you. May we make that connection?

R. Yes.

D. Diana here with you, Rose. I am not going to use you for the work of being my only voice, but you are indeed a very focal point of my work. Do not feel that there is a way for you to escape the fact that I chose you first and foremost as the one that I communicated with. You were a wicked good channel and a very delight to communicate with, and the fact that I have chosen Andrew for his vocal connection skills is not to reflect at all upon your work as one who can hear me. My thoughts are very refined in your mind, and that is indeed a vast source of glee for me.

I am ever with you as the ones you speak to now, and I wanted only to pop in and confirm for you that you are indeed to be my channel, my voice as it were, and nothing has changed in that agreement you and I had from the beginning.

I am aware that confusion reigns within you as to your role in my plans, and that will be made abundantly clear in very short shrift from now.

I am ever working to align some things that need to be revealed, and I would prefer that you never again refer to the fact that my work with you is finished.

It is not, my dear, nor will it ever be as long as you are in favor of allowing me to speak with you. I am not ready to reveal even to my channels the fullness of my plans, but I am pre-pared to step forward and offer you this: I am an ever-loyal person to those who are loyal to me. I have been well graced with the loyalty of you and the others.

There are a few others who have deserted me and my words to them, but when there is a riper fullness to my plans, then there may be a joining again of my mind with theirs.

Let not the time that goes by with no word from me ever create in you a doubt of my intentions of my loyalty to you. There will be a given moment when your connection to me shall shine as brightly as that of Andrew and Marcia and another of whom I am using.

Of this, I am giving my pledge. You have served me faith-fully and have served my other voices faithfully as well. Let us remember the friendship we had while doing my book, and I will ever be your friend as I had promised. You have shown yourself a friend of mine, and that is my greatest gift from you.

While your voice is indeed needed for my work, it is your friendship that is needed for the doer of that work. Thank you for allowing me these moments in your time with your counselors. I am ever yours.

R. Thank you, Diana. I had intended to speak to you later any-way, and I am cheered by your words and glad you came to me. I again make my pledge to do what I can for your work as I did when I chose to do your book. As I say to my physical friends, "We be cool, baby!" Thank you.

Back to my guides...so I can work with Diana and others?

MLK: TREATISES FROM MY LIFE

G. As we have said from the beginning, you may choose to work with all that you deem of wanting to, and we will facilitate the connection if they are also willing. You have at your access all who reside in this world. Has not our connection to you of the others made this clear? If you could but see the line of those waiting to speak through you, you would be overwhelmed and overloaded, but it is our function to allow only those who you give permission for.

We are the gatekeepers, but you are the key master. You are the one who has final say as to the thrust of the work upon your world. Do you have a request for us now?

R. I do. I would like again to speak to Martin. I want to begin some work with him as well. I admire him and am thinking of doing a book on him. Is he available?

G. There is no need to ask if he is available. There is no such thing as not being available within this world. There are no pressing reasons that one cannot do many things at once, and he is indeed eager to have your attention. Speak to him as he is with you.

R. Martin, how are you?

MARTIN. I am elated that you have been perusing my life and my work. I am ever eager to be of service to those who need a voice for the raising of them from their cages of injustice, be it the cage of prejudice, poverty, power inequalities, or any form of repression. I am ever ready to bring my passion and presence to the fore for those who need it.

I was once a powerful man within your world, and that will never change. However, I am now but a personality with no voice that may resound upon your world except through those who feel my spirit of love for the undoing of all shackles that may bind the heart and soul.

I would welcome your decision to do a book based on my life or, most importantly, my death. What the world does not know are the moments when I left that world, left my family, and the purging in my spirit that accompanied that leaving of your world. I would indeed be quite honored if you would give me a forum for that.

I have thought many times of making a reentrance to your world but as of yet have not chosen to do so. I am ever sorely troubled by the things I see and have thought the thoughts of reentering to serve again in a body for those who still feel the bite of shackles upon them. The way is being shown in many sectors of the world for the removal of some shackles, but the arm of hatred is still around the throats of far too many.

I would welcome a chance to deliver a series of treatises on that and other subjects and would be honored if you would serve me as a form of secretary, not to diminish your gifts as it were but as a figure of speech.

I have no hands with which to write as I once did. I have no voice to fill an auditorium. I have no feet upon which to march. But I do have a spirit with which to feel the cries of the repressed and the hated. I have a mind with which to formulate solutions and soul-utions.

Let that pun be a gentle reminder that the soul of not only the haters but the hated are being scarred and that the bite of hatred is ever infecting the heart of the world.

Would you be my secretary? Become my voice with raging volume? Would you serve as the spokesperson for one

MLK: TREATISES FROM MY LIFE

who left that world through the hatred and fear of another through the machinations of many?

I am ready to reveal many things that would affect the planet and the balance of power that has reigned through fear and anger. It will not be a comfortable position, I fear, for I am not an easy being to deal with. I am burning, even yet with indignation, over the things that have not changed in decades— the things that have existed for centuries. The solutions that I presented while there were profound in the idea of peace and though accused of stealing those ideas, I do yet feel the power of them.

I am not asking that you abandon your other work. I would not take your skills from the others who have work as important as mine, but if you would serve as my typist, I will set down some treatises that would help serve the purpose of my work and aid the work of the others.

Diana was a woman of love and affection. Make no mistake. I am not so gentle in my demeanor as she had ever been.

I am fired up, I am indignant, I am possessed! The work you do with me will not be so flowery and so easy to sell. It will offend many. It will blast from the fields and the gullies those who are empowered through the use of fear and hatred. It will remove the chaff from the wheat, and the blowby will be virulent. I will make the ways clean again if I have the means to do so.

R.   What do you think I can do for you? I haven't had much luck getting Diana's words out there. They sat in my computer for years. Why do you think I will have any better luck with your work when you warn me it will offend many?

M.   You aren't worried about your safety? You aren't worried about your reputation? That is a good sign for me, for my cause does not warrant the use of those who walk in fear.

But to answer your question, I will repeat myself. You are not to be the one whose words will be given. I will make it clear that the words are from me as your friend is going to do.

You will serve only in capacity of typist. I will make the words clear in their meaning. I will make sure that the proper sources for you are made available to further my work. I will not allow you to sit idle as you have done in your other work. You will be made over into a heart of fire as well.

Your courage and spirit will hold up well for my work, and I would see to it that it works for the good of all. I am no longer focused only on the cause of racial injustice. I am fired up for the souls of man, which bear no color.

Your participation will be only as that which fills the lack of my voice. You will not be harmed and will not be made accountable for my opinions.

Of this, I would guarantee. Many will be the things that will be said that will only have my ring of authenticity. There will be no blurring of my energy with yours and no crossing of my thoughts to yours, except for this work of recording my thoughts for these articles I intend to write.

Let no man make the mistake of thinking that I can be stopped from this world! I am sincere in my intent with this and need to know if you are the one to do this.

R.   I am interested. I wonder though how you think you can offer me protection. You didn't even protect yourself while here, did you now?

MLK: TREATISES FROM MY LIFE

But this is a different world from then. While I realize that many will not agree, I have faith that I would not be harmed unless I had given permission for it on a spiritual level anyway.

The offer of your protection, while noted and appreciated, is not a concern. If I am to do the work that I have been told I am to do, then I have the protection of others in the spirit realm as well.

I am comfortable with that thought. But if I do this thing, do choose to be your *typist*, then you had better make sure you get your act together to get someone in line with me to get it out there. My role is as a channel…not PR and advertising. Is that understood?

M. You are a hard woman, Miss Rose. I would agree. You will need not worry with the how of it, just with what is said and how it gets to paper. But I am in possession of information that makes the way clear to me of how this is to get done. Leave that to me and think about being at my command for a good while.

R. How long is a *good while*?

M. I have a series of articles that I want written—articles that may work as well for magazine print and radio and as well as for a book. We will be with these for some time. I will offer an estimate of six months to one year, depending upon your ability to type and make room for me in your schedule.

I have no pressing need to make you work for free, you understand? That would be against some of things I stood for, do you realize?

But I also do not want this to become a work of immense wealth to you either.

23

I have no need for the monetary value of this work. It is for the value to souls that I offer this, but it is not for you to suffer from poverty when you have the means of your own hands to raise you from that.

It is part and parcel of my message from my time on your earth. So do this with me, join me in my fire, and let us liberate the souls held in bondage. You may accept monetary reward for it, and that is fine.

It is even desired by me. But let me warn that if you succumb to greed and avarice as those whom we will be targeting, your life will not be comfortable there or here. Does that resonate with your idea of a black man who once hated being paid by his skin color? Who watched the greed suck the life dry out of those who worked to make life comfortable for those of another skin color? Earning a fair wage is desirable. Bleeding a soul never is.

Think of this: Confirm it with your spouse. I would never have had my moment in the limelight if I had not had Coretta's backing.

I am aware of the bond that exist between a man's or a woman's homelife and their work in the world outside a home.

I often stretched the bonds of mine, and I would not ask that of you. But do this thing and serve not only me but also the world at large, for my words are destined to ring from the microphones again in that world.

We will speak again. I am ever ready and ever eager.

R.   Thank you, Martin. I will get back with you.

MLK: TREATISES FROM MY LIFE

Ultimately, I did get back with Martin, agreed to the arrangements, and set aside some time each week for dictation. What follows from here are his treatises, his words.

I may write a conclusion, but then again, I may just let what he gave us settle in with you.

I will see what spirit moves me to do. If you read the entire book, then you too will discover what I decide to do.

Ladies and gentlemen, Martin Luther King Jr.

THE RESISTANCE OF FEAR

For those of you who fear death, let me speak now to still that fear. My name, as you would know it, is Martin Luther King Jr., and I am gone from that world but surely not dead as to what is happening there.

I come again to speak, to educate, and to eradicate the bonds that would hold men in slavery—not the slavery that my forebears fought against but forms of slavery that ensnare all men despite their color, creed, or convictions.

I am still singing the praises of freedom and am ever still fired up over that cause, but I am not limited in my sight as I once was. My vision of freedom now is beyond what I could have seen when I was there. Fear not, children of God, for I have come again to speak to the ears of those who care to hear.

In the minds of men, there are always many aspects of fear. The greatest of these being the issues of survival.

I have understood that the root of all fear is the issue of survival, and for this reason, I am well incensed that the ones who control through use of fear are willing to erase the survival of someone else to ensure their own.

These findings of human nature are not but borne out in the Bible, for the tale is as old as humans themselves.

However, the plight of those who have been made to bear the brunt of the fears of others has also a fear of survival within them. In these reactions to the fears well imbedded in man lies the result of unrest. Are there to be a releasing of the fears of all man, then shall there be a resting of all unrest.

MLK: TREATISES FROM MY LIFE

My pleas to that world upon my living there is for it to release those who hold down by fear of equality. Many have been the strides in that department since my death, but how mighty the sword that still must be wielded to hack the last of those fears from the minds of men.

I am sore displaced from that world; no longer do I walk among you. However, even in my present state, do I feel the cries of those who bear the burden of injustice—injustices caused by the fears in men's minds?

I walk now in a new way, march as it is to a new cause. I am utilizing the hands of one of your world to make my statements and will be ever so grateful if you treated this one with respect as to her position as my typist.

Her mind is not formulating the words; it is my thoughts that are given and her fingers that type them.

If your qualms are with the words, do not misplace your venom upon the typist. She has agreed to fill this position out of caring for my former work and for my current habit of asking her to do so.

I am not representing her, and she is not representing me. Her function is solely as typist. The thoughts within are my own, and that will become soon self-evident.

I was torn from my work in my earlier life at a young age—an age that would see most flourishing and living life to the fullest. I was dedicated to my work at a great expense to my private life.

I had much regret to bear for my former actions that cost me the respect of some and the fullness of the trust of my wife Coretta, a finer woman there who had not been and a very large part of my success.

Had Coretta not believed in a lowly preacher with an elevated cause, I would not and could not have endured the trail.

I was gone often from my family, and they lost much of who I was and how I loved them. I felt my children would be there when the trail ended, and I had miscalculated. The trail ended upon a cold and windy balcony, and I had no chance to see or hold them again.

I was prepared to take my work to the end of my life, and even though I knew that that end might come at any moment, I was not prepared at that exact moment.

I was looking over the railing at friends, listening to their voices when a man filled with fear, and loathing took my life. It was not he who acted alone, for there were many in that room with him. No, I do not speak in riddles, for when a man carries a function out such as that, he carries the fear of many in his mind.

His was not the only fear that ended my life that day, but also it was the fear and machinations of many—of the many who lost sight of their own humanity and had no course of sight with which to regain it.

I am ever sorely pressed to understand the harm done to my family in that moment. I am ever sorely pressed to relive that moment.

I was filled with a fire of determination and the warm glow of friendship. I was filled with the thought of a wonderful evening of food and drink. I was not thinking that in a moment, I would lie bleeding upon the ground and dying to that world. It was perhaps a wonderful way to go; had it not been for the pain.

In those moments, as I lost control of life, not for the first time surely but for the final time certainly, I was filled with fear myself. Fear that I was dying. Fear that my wife would see me shattered. Fear that my children would have no father and no support with things they would need. I had fear that my work would die then and there. Oh, how mighty the fear when one is left dying through the fear of another!

I was taken back to a memory—a memory of a time when I was about ten, and the words of a man to an acquaintance of mine made me realize that not all of us were well-liked and respected.

It was my introduction to the harsh realities of that world. I was dying, and my final thoughts were of the hatred that another had for a child because he was not the same as him.

Yes, that was my final thought, and perhaps I was taken there in my last conscious thoughts before entering the heavens so that

MLK: TREATISES FROM MY LIFE

I would take my work with me to the next world! I am sorely pressed to remember that moment.

The will of that man who wielded a rifle to kill me had not begun that morning nor had it begun that year. It began with the first thought of someone to hate someone else who was different than they were.

It was a culmination of many years, decades, and centuries of fear. I was but the outward sign of one who embodied the voice of reason. I was but a target of the internal fears of many men.

My death was not a personal thing. That man had never had cross words with me. That man was not a man who would kill for that reason. But kill he did for his way of life for him and his own.

It was pure fear that pulled that trigger, not a rational mindset on being one with others who had a different color of skin. I am sore pressed now to reveal the role of such fear in many domains upon that world.

When I was leaving my body and grasping at staying, I felt the chill of certainty coming over me that I was futilely working at something that would show no results. I was taken as if by the lapel and lifted up and over my own self. I was hurled into a state of flux and waves of wonder as I realized I had lost the battle. I was not there, and yet I was! I was not alone, and yet there was no one with me! I felt lifted, and yet a burden descended around me as I realized I was gone from that body.

I knew that no more would I be seen or heard and never again to hold my babies. I was indeed a man but yet not a man. I was alive and yet not in a body. I was aware of the rush of emotions of others, my own a jumble of thoughts and reactions.

I faced the greatest fear ever of where was I and what was to become of me. I had not envisioned my entering the heavens as being one of such upheaval.

It was a sad time, and yet a jubilation was being infused into me as if from another source.

When a man faces his fear of death, as I did on that cold floor, you realize how great the fear in a man can be.

I was not a coward. I had proved that many a time by placing myself in the hands of the Lord and marching into the lion's den.

I was not one to flee but rather one to march onward. However, in that moment when I knew that death was there staring me in the face, I would have run if I had had the power to do so. I would have buckled to fear and did what I would not thought possible of me. I would have bargained with the devil to be left alive!

But you might say, "Surely as a man of the Lord, you had no fear of dying and being rewarded!"

I tell you now that even with my understanding that the Lord wanted me to do as I did, I would have kissed the devil himself to have gotten to live.

The idea of a reward for services rendered was not a thought in my consciousness in those moments. It was pure fear, and that is the point of my thesis today.

Fear is a strong motivator, and I hold forth on a discussion of this through the woman who agreed to type my words.

I was not a believer that man had no use for eternity. I was myself ever driven to do the work I felt had been given to me for the purchase of a plot of eternity. I was not a man who ran from his duties but one who felt that duty was payment upon the land he would inhabit in eternity. I was, in my mind, purchasing a plot of ground in the kingdom with which to retire to. I had that in my mind even as I marched for the freedom of others.

Was that a self-serving motivation? Perhaps, but it is an honest statement.

I felt I had the calling, and to shirk my duty would have been unthinkable to me.

I was ever pressed to flow forward, and the flow was ever-widening. I was not always given to know where I would be taken upon the flow, but the flow always presented itself to me, and I knew that I had to follow. I marched as the flow dictated, and the voice resounded within me.

Yes, I said the voice. I was not one to hear voices, but I did hear a voice. It was the voice that calmed me, upheld me, and made

MLK: TREATISES FROM MY LIFE

me more than I would have been without its timber echoing in my head.

I was not a follower of the idea that the Lord spoke to everyone, but I did feel that I was being led by the Lord through the use of that voice. Perhaps I felt that because I was a minister, I had a special relationship with the voice. Perhaps I had no other answer for it. But follow that voice I did. It held me to the task, and I answered in action as best I could.

If your answer to my thoughts is that you have never heard the voice, then be aware that I am given to know that the voice resides in us all now.

I was wrong to assume I had a special relationship with that voice. It is proof and certainty of my ego and how I made a mockery of that voice by assuming that I was special.

I had heard it only when I needed. I was seeking it only after I had come to a low point in my life and had need of it.

I have no doubt now that the voice had spoken many times before, but my first listening was when I was sore pressed to continue with the burdens I had come to bear. But once the voice is heard, the ear is open, and the way can be seen.

I offer this to you from this level I now dwell in for I would correct the misconception that I had that only the selected few may hear the voice. I was wrong, and those who teach that dogma are wrong.

The Lord does not choose favorites! I was not a recipient of that voice because I was a minister, but because I was a man seeking it.

I was not a chosen one of God; I had chosen God to help me in that moment. Do you hear what I was saying? Do you understand the words of a spirit who wants to correct the misconceptions even I held as a man?

Do not make the mistake that I did by assuming you have no power to hear that voice. It indwells us as surely as it indwelled the Christ! Amen, and the truth must be told!

The truth of fear is that it can make a man do and be the things he never would have thought himself possible. Would I have considered myself a man who would have fought going to my Lord? No, indeed, I had not. Would I have been a man who would have entertained trading my plot of eternity for a mere few years on the earth? No, sir, I was not that man, not at all until the time arrived and fear grabbed me by the throat and made me a man I had never envisioned. It is a truth that fear is a great manipulator of men.

I was not a man who would have been afraid of the man who pulled the trigger, had I met him. I am aware that he was a good man within his own mind. He was a good man within his circle of family and friends. It was not that he was born a killer nor was he a man who had entertained killing for most of his life.

I am aware that he even had a mind that could have challenged mine, had we the occasion to speak to one another as men. But the fear that resided in him, that cold hard core of fear, was the killer. It was the manipulator that brought him to the edge that he would have not envisioned himself being at had that world been different.

My family recognized the good in that man. They had seen his soul and his fear. They knew that he worked not with his heart on that day but with his mind of fear.

They knew too well the price of fear, for they had felt it. They had been more than once in its sway. That was why forgiveness is to be found in them for someone who thought he was doing right when fear had him in its clutches.

My point here with this treatise is this: Fear is an insidious form of control. It is a far-reaching malady in the world. *It* is the root cause of things not sanctioned of God. *It* is the antithesis of love, which is the energy of God. *It* is the reason I died and the reason men die all over the world even today.

How does fear, in its manifestation, enter the hearts of God-fearing men and women? How does fear make its debut in the hearts of those attuned to the life that has been offered them if they are but steadfast in their ways of walking in love?

This is the answer I strive to give to you, to my children, and to the world that still lives in fear rather than love. This answer

MLK: TREATISES FROM MY LIFE

will correct many things I had tried to do when I walked there as a man. It is the answer that I sought and did not find. Only after facing those moments on the balcony did I get a true appreciation of what fear can do to a man; even a man possessed of the love for brother.

The answer is deep. The answer is wide. The answer is higher than the greatest mind can fathom if it is not entered into the full kingdom of love. That is why I reach back now, my brothers and sisters, and offer that answer. It is the answer; I had found it in my life as a man there when I led others toward freedom from restriction, which would have turned the tide sooner and more completely. It is where I failed as a great leader, and I bear no qualms at admitting that regardless of the thoughts that others might have of me as that man. I was not a leader from fear and toward love but rather an instiller of more fear.

Yes, I know that it is not an easy thing that I admit. I was not a man possessed of the love that needed to be given. I was possessed, and I did burn with great fire to relieve the suffering of others, but I was possessed of fighting fear with the propagation of more fear.

Oh yeah, I did have love in my heart. I did find ways to try and fight violence with nonviolence. I did walk as a man possessed of the right cause. These things I will not dispute.

However, the underlying tentacle that propelled me is fear—fear that I did not fully admit to or recognize until that time when I had to part that world and saw myself as that child witnessing the fear of a man spewing forth hate to a child who feared his difference and feared the man's anger. I was the child who witnessed this and felt both fears. Not being old enough to recognize the fear of the man I did not consciously equate his anger with fear.

I did relate to the child's fear and my own fear of being hated. I remember I walked home a changed being, realizing that I was not loved by all and that my world was limited by hate and anger. I was mournful of that but did not realize the roots of fear that had been instilled in me and the anger that would give birth to in many years' time.

Had I been a man who had not chosen to walk the path of ministry as I did and am now aware of what I was led to do, then my birth of anger would have been perhaps more violent. I would have found myself in a room with a rifle one day perhaps.

The difference between I who lived my life and the man who ended my life is that I found diverse ways to channel my fear and anger. I was led by God to find the idea of nonviolence and that became my armor to keep fear and anger from being what it could have been.

Had it not been for my prompting to take that path, I could have, and most undoubtedly would have, been a very frightening man full of fear and anger. But for the grace of God, there go I as the old saying goes.

Now you wonder why I admit to such tentacles of fear being the foundation of my peaceful work. Let me clarify the methodology that was in my mind at that time and how I could not see the tentacles that had wound themselves into my very fibers as a human, but that seem so clear now.

I was not a fan of violence ever. I had been the recipient of violence and knew that the use of it instilled fear. It was not a thing that felt good to my soul. When I became aware of the work of others who recognized the inherent wrong of forcing others to live in fear of harm and mental bondage, I was struck by that ideology.

However, I read the message but not the fine print. I did not see that to carry that message forth with fear in my heart would be a sin, as it was, of magnifying that which was not intended. It was as if a man had planted a seed but forgot to till the soil, and the seed died in the hardened soil.

My heart was that hardened soil. It was a place of deep fear and roiling anger over being fearful.

The seed of nonviolence was planted in a soil that harbored the fungus of fear, don't you see?

Taking that seed, I became enamored of that ideology. I wanted to use that seed and plant other fields of it in a broader scope.

MLK: TREATISES FROM MY LIFE

I wanted to be a nonviolent farmer, as it was, reliving the ways of my grandfather in a metaphorical way. I wanted to till the soil of action without violence.

When presented the platform with which to use that seed, I gathered my tools and ran forth, eager to be a sower of that seed. It was a rightful ideology but a wrongful approach. Why? Because while I advocated the use of nonviolence by one section, I was guilty of utilizing the violence of another section to further my work. I even gave it code names to justify the use of it.

I knew well that the fear in men's hearts of our work and our messages would spark violence, given the right fertilizer. I knew where that fertilizer was stored. It was stored in the hearts and minds of other men, just as it was stored in my own. But my own, I could deny if I was busy sowing nonviolent fields, don't you see?

Had I been a man given to more self-examination and truth of my own deep fears, I would never have undertaken the using of other men's fears as fertilizer to launch my own work of nonviolent resistance.

It was a wrongful act and one that did not yield the best crop of love. It did yield results, and many good things did come to pass from it, and yet in reflection of that time and those means, I am sore pressed to admit that my own folly was in leading in the use of other men's fears. It is not something I would sanction today, given what I have come to learn about the true nature of fear and love.

So where does the core of fear come from? Where does fear reproduce and spread its tentacles from one heart to another? Here is the answer: Let us go back as it was to the beginning.

Being a man of ministry, I was taught the works of many great thinkers. I was inundated with scripture. I was given the best that man knew of that time to produce in man a spirit of love of God and man. However, I now see that the use of these things were but a mockery of the real truth. They were, as it was, the purveyors of fear.

If one looks at the role that man had in the Bible as a starting point for my soliloquy, then we see that man fell from grace through fear. Not love, but fear. It was fear of missing something and fear of truth being hidden from him.

I need not quote or expound upon the scripture. All those of the Christian faith know of this fall from grace. Once that fear had taken hold and they left the grace of pure love, then they found the fears of survival.

The tale of the rocky and barren soil is the tale of fear of survival. Their connection with pure love had been altered when fear entered the picture. The tale of leaving that garden of pure love shows the entry of fear in other ways.

Fear has cost us our grace and children, and the way back is only through the finding of pure love again.

How has fear grown? How has fear reigned in all countries, religious systems, and minds and hearts? What method does fear use to seed itself and spread like a choking weed through the world? That is the real cause of wars, bondage, harm, and killing of another. Where has this weed been given root?

The art form of instilling fear has been around as long as man. The story of the serpent, that vile creature that tempted the man who had nothing but love within him, was nothing short of a gilded tale about the ego mind versus the loving heart.

The heart of man knew neither right nor wrong, for there was only perfection within them. However, as man grew in that perfection, their minds became imbued with the idea that maybe they were missing something. That something was not as it seemed to them, and that if they listened to their minds, that more could be added to their world. That fear of missing something has never left man to this day.

When humans began to multiply, not only their numbers but also their ideas of what could be, then man began to harness the power of thought to see what they could have that they did not already have.

Herein enters greed to the minds of men. The analogy of Cain and Abel was only removed from the perfect form of man in his garden of love by one generation, and yet greed had taken hold

MLK: TREATISES FROM MY LIFE

of men's minds. It was the story of how fear allowed a man to kill his brother and to kill the hope that had been within that human form for other generations.

Fear was the root of that killing as surely as fear had been at the root of my own. Fear was and is the finger that pulled the proverbial triggers.

Had I known that my inducing fear so greatly into the minds of men would multiply that force, I would have trodden a very different path. But you see, I did not recognize the force of fear in me and therefore could not see that my actions were spearheaded by the anger in me for having been made to fear.

In my righteous mode of thinking, I felt that the means justified the cause. It did not, my fellow brethren, for had I used the power of love instead of inducing fear, I would have found a much greater sight from that mountaintop I had spoken of climbing. I would have seen the glory of love reinstated with no fear as an inductor of action.

In a battle of wills concerning the human condition, the power of fear often replaces love, and this is the foresight I did not have on my journey to the promised land.

I was like Moses; I tried to lead the people into the promised land—a land I had been promising them. However, like Moses, I could only stumble in circles, for my power came not from pure love as I had supposed but from the hidden agenda of fear placed into me by another who had been taught to fear. And so I taught others to fear as well.

This was not a moment to unload the burden of my soul, though it was from reflection that I saw I was liable for that action. It was a warning, a cry from me to the world that I misled and who had yet to fully find that promised land that I spoke so eloquently of.

My powers as a leader and orator were well served but not for the result that could have been. What if I had been a true teacher of love, a true Messiah, as some liked to call me? What if I had been a man with no anger and fear instilled in me? Would I have understood that to elevate the levels of fear were wrong? Would I have stood by and allowed the children to feel fear and feel the anger of the crowds? Would I have been the man who marched others into harm's way and allowed the use of fear and weapons?

I am not a man any longer in the world of bodies, but I am a soul who needs to correct the mistakes of that man who marched proudly and led others into a war of fear against fear.

Let the Lord be my witness, and the angels bear testimony to the fact that I have come forward not to cleanse my soul, though the result may well be that, but rather to cry out into the wilderness known as fear and hate that I was but the one who made way for the time of love.

I have no agenda, I have no greater glory, I am not but a servant—the servant I should have been had I cleansed my own house before trying to cleanse the houses of others.

It is my privilege to have a means to be that servant, and I am blessed to have found one who can deliver my sermon as it was to those who still do not understand the filth of fear in their own hearts and minds.

I was a man of the cloth, a minister, a preacher, an orator, and a man possessed to correct those things of injustice. I took seriously my vows, my duties, and my causes. I was not a glory seeker, though it was a by-product of my work. I was not a man pressed to be wealthy or famous, but I was a man pressed to be known for my righteous anger over unjust causes.

For those who claimed I sought the glory for myself, I can answer that with the reminder that glory does not come with a jail sentence.

Glory does not come with having bombs thrown at your family and innocent children. No, glory does not pay well enough to cost the lives of my beloved children or the children of others. It was not for glory, not for money, not for anything earthly that I did what I did. It was because I believed.

I believed that I had a calling—a special calling to be the front-runner for those who lacked the courage, the ideology of nonviolence to use against the hands that held them.

MLK: TREATISES FROM MY LIFE

I had the Voice and it called me to step forward, to not retreat, to never grow weary, and flag at my duties. It pummeled me into action, and I, therefore, pummeled others into action as well.

Those who followed me believed. Those who came after me believed. Oh, but had we only known what I was shown upon that balcony that day as my own force of work ended! Had we only known that the wages of fear I had been instrumental in earning was being paid in full by the hand of the man who had listened to my own fear and responded. Had we only used love instead of fear, our work would have paid much richer rewards!

Am I alone in my sin? Am I the sole reason that man did as he did? Was I alone playing the role of serpent to the others I worked against?

No, I did not alone bear that burden. I am clear in myself that I was not the only cause. I was but one segment of a unit of a nation of a world that fed into that man's actions. I was but a cog in the machinations that lead to such acts.

Had that man been born to fear? No, no babe is fearful of a man's skin color or a man's economic worth or potential. That is a learned condition.

Was that man a child who grew up dreaming of the time he could kill another? No, that man was a child with only thoughts of fun and frivolity in his young mind. Had he been a teen more interested in politics than girls? I doubt not. He was just what we all are: a person taught to fear through family, education, religion, and nationality. These are the purveyors of fear and the monsters under the beds of all adult humans.

I was a man, as I said before, who did not look under my bed. I did not realize that I even had a monster lurking within me.

How many of you realize this? How many of you, my fellow children of God, have the monster of fear tucked neatly under your bed and are too afraid to look for that monster?

If any answer in the truth of the Lord, they must admit that there is fear there within them. It is a relative thing, this fear. It might be a big hairy fear, or it might be a small fuzzy fear, but it

ROSE CAMPBELL

is a fear nonetheless. It is an insidious manipulator no matter the size or the content.

Which of us who have stood upon a pulpit have not taught the fear of reprisal or condemnation for acts perceived by us as being against God? Who has not felt the subliminal messages of patriotism that our country is better than and that all others must be defended against? What form of education does not teach that to fail is to condemn you to a failed life?

The purveyors of fear do not recognize the fear they spread. It is packaged, labeled, promoted, and accepted without there ever being a thorough check on the foundations of what is being sold. It is a state of existence that exists to propagate fear without the normal man or woman ever seeing the monster for what it is and what it is not.

If religions teach that the effects of sin is reprisals, then what of those religions who do not recognize our own standards of moral decision? What if they do not accept our version of deity? Do they not teach their own members the same resounding ideology that to not be united against those who are not worshippers as we are of the same deity that there will be hell to pay?

I use that word *hell* with great aplomb, for it was a word I was well-familiar with as a man. It was a word that I, as a leader of religious men, used to instill fear in my flock and the community as best I could. It was what I was taught, it was what I accepted, and it was what I dispensed.

Yes, I sometimes shouted the word, sometimes it was hinted, and more often than not it was implied by the contrast given between heaven for the righteous and the fate of those who did not walk righteously.

But the idea was to fear that if you walked other than as was accepted by your own brand of deity worship that the results would be dire, should the word *hell* be used directly or not. Oh yes, religion is a bona fide purveyor of fear, and these fears reside under many a bed.

What could the outcome of two groups who worship quite differently be if the fear that is harbored in their hearts is fanned as I fanned the fear of racial and economic disturbances within a system? Do you still find it hard to believe that humans would turn against one another in wars waged over theological dissention, knowing that each teach the other wrong and that acceptance of that other way would condemn you to dire consequences? Do you not see the seeds of fear igniting into terminal chaos? See that monster, my brethren? Hear it breathing under your own bed.

What of a system that teaches that because you walk, breathe, love, and work in such and such a place that your life is better than those who do these things in another location? That your way of life, be it within a powerful developed nation or a nation of ancient ways, is to be defended at all costs. What if your leaders said that even before another group came to your land that you must be proactive and go there to head them off in case they wanted to come to your land? What of the man who shirks his duty for his country and does not defend her? What is thought of that man? Are they not ridiculed, ostracized, and even imprisoned? Are not men denied access to their own land again simply for abiding by a rule taught by their religious leaders that to kill would bring upon them dire consequences? Which fear should they purchase? Which fear holds the most power over them?

Listen closely, children. There are two breathing monsters under the bed.

Having spent many years in the halls of learning, I was an avid student of the fear of failing. I walked on campuses and heard the monster's breath but did not pay attention to the sound. It was a very low sound, and few around me seemed to hear it either, not for what it really was. But the effect was the same on those who knew it and those who did not.

It was the slow and repetitive equation of self with what appeared on a scorecard. Never mind that some were brilliant mathematicians while others were equally brilliant with languages—all had to pass everything to be found worthy.

It proved you worthy of entry to the next level of education, the next good job, even the consideration as a good potential spouse. But what of those who did not acquire a place among those in the halls of higher learning? Were they unworthy as men and women because they repaired cars or grew vegetables or toiled with the hands to provide needed services? If they were of certain racial or economic backgrounds, how could they prove themselves in the eyes of academia if they were unacceptable of entry due to these factors?

Those of you familiar with my life know that I fought as well for the right to education for those who had been denied all but the most meager of learning situations. I saw the beast; I had even felt its jaws around my throat when I was denied joining my white peers once we began to go to school. I saw the difference then, but it was not until later that I felt the fear packaged for me by the educational systems and the beliefs in that system.

My self-worth as a man, especially as a black man, rode on what was handed to me upon a piece of paper. My worthiness was defined by my power to learn what others had decided would be beneficial for me to know no matter what I already knew from my own connection with life.

I was a lucky man in my day. I had the economic structure to afford schooling. I was able to find schools that would take a black man and could afford to make education my priority in my youth. But was I wiser than my noneducated counterparts? Was I more worthy of respect? Did I deserve a better job with no family while a man with a family, but no paper showing his achievements, shined my shoes? What fear that division caused for those not as lucky as I! To be judged unworthy of many things due to a lack of scholastic achievements is indeed a great purveyor of fear.

Thank my Lord that some things have changed since my day as a man there. No longer does the achievements you garner bear a direct correlation to the color of your skin or the size of your daddy's wallet.

Yes, it still exists to a degree, but the way is clearing every year for those things to fade away.

The advent of loans to students of all classes has done much to equate the mind with its true measure, not the measure of your heritage and the jingle in your pocket. Hallelujah, and I say amen to that!

But do you see now the causes and the tentacles of fear I am getting at? Do you smell the foul breath that seeps from under many a man's proverbial bed? Do you understand the fullness of my claims that these fears are taught and not inborn? That all of us, even though of the highest striving to be men of God, are guilty of spreading the thing that caused us the loss of grace?

Hear me now: There is no sin in anything but in allowing fear to overcome the love.

God is love, and I swear to you that is the truest statement written in any text.

In my moment of greatest fear, the moment when I knew I was dying and all I had worked for and loved would be mine no longer, I saw and I knew. I saw the fear, and I knew that I had been wrong, not wrong in my desires but wrong in my methods, and that I had been one to use fears given me and contort them into something to bring fear to others. I knew then I had sinned.

The wisdom that a man could not find his own way through the world without the benefit of religion, patriotic zeal, and formal education was a slow time coming; but when the idea took hold, it did so with a vengeance.

The time of my forefathers when they were free in a land that knew no such tenets was a time of greater connection to the Voice I had spoken of. They found their way through listening to their inner wisdoms. They fought for survival—that is true, but they were not unhappy people.

I had spoken to many who wished we had never left those lands, whether it happened through force or under their own powers. However, I say to each of you who have desired a return to your forefather's countries: *Do not* be rushed in your efforts to return to a place that no longer exists. The lands of freedom of those things no longer exist within your world.

There is no nirvana to be found by going back. It is the same and will always be changing. That is life on your world.

The way to that promised land I spoke of is not to board ships and planes and embark upon a journey back into time. That time no longer exists, my people, and so do not mourn for something that is not real.

The way to find the promised land is within your grasp wherever you may be, whatever vocation you find yourselves in, and whenever you see the light of love as a beacon.

I was a man who saw that land, but it was not a real land—a land made of dirt and rocks. It was a land within the minds of men. It was a time to come when all will live as brothers even unto the plains of Mississippi.

There is no greater land than the land of men in harmony with one another. Do not take my words as a man there with a literal understanding. I was not advocating a return to the motherland. I was advocating a return to the garden of love.

In my clarity that I have come to know now, not as a man of the world of flesh but as a soul in the plains of all knowledge, I see where I went wrong. I see where I came from and where I was leading others.

It is my form of redemption to come now through the use of another, to speak again from the podium of leadership to correct my vision, and to correct my path that I would lead you upon. If any who reads these words feel they are for the men only of color, they are wrong. If they feel it is only for the oppressed that I speak again, they are in error.

I speak to all men, and by that term, I am using the generic version since I refer to all human life, male and female. My words do not exclude; they include. My words are not beacons to the inhabitants of one land or country over another. They are for the world and the souls of all who possess the intelligence to hear the truth in them.

My voice once rang out over the masses for some time a while ago. That same voice used to stir the imaginations and hearts of thousands.

MLK: TREATISES FROM MY LIFE

My goal now is to reach the ones who have never seen me speak, as well as those who are old enough to remember my visual image upon their television screens.

It is for all that I come forth and speak again. It is for all that I have enlisted the aid of a secretary and a fine one at that.

Her work with me is not her platform, and it is not of her origin. It is I, the soul of Martin Luther King Jr., who speaks through these words. Do not make the mistake of thinking that once I died that my intent to be a man of the Lord and of the people died with me.

Each of you will one day know the truth of what I say: To leave that world does not preclude the burn in your soul for your highest goals upon that world. The truth is that you do feel, you do see, and do care with even more intensity.

It is something I learned through the use of another man's bullet. My body died that day, but my soul was imbued with even more fire, more clarity, and more will to see my work of freeing people continue. However, with that event, I saw the ways in which I had to change that work.

I am now here to amend my former leadership and fine-tune my directions to the promised land.

There are never any good ways to uproot the fears from inside a man when they are hidden. The man alone must do that form of work. However, to post signs that say, "Here is fear," "Here is the way fear shows itself" is the best that I can do. Let me return to posting my signs.

I have touched upon the purveyors of fear. Those institutions that are seldom questioned and examined for the basis of their beliefs are often the greatest hiders of fear.

Take a look at your affiliations. Take a hard look at the core beliefs of your alliances. Question the ways in which they segregate and separate.

Take not another man's word that the way is truth; seek that knowledge for yourself. Do not be as a lamb led to the slaughter, but as a lion, which lets no man lead him to his death.

Brook no excuses for the behaviors that would create harm and chaos. Turn not from one human as if they are less than you. Never think of yourself as a more chosen of God, for God is not partial to any of his children.

Does it matter if one child calls his father *Daddy* and another calls his daddy *Poppa*? Does it matter if one man calls his deity *God* while another calls him *Allah*?

Think now, Brothers! Think now, Sisters! Do any of you have questions? Do any of you have nagging doubts in your hearts about those things you follow? Does anything in your world point to a way that divides and conquers, separates and segregates? Are you following something or someone because you are too lazy to find your own answers? Do you follow what you are told to follow as children and have not used your adult mind to sift through the truth for yourself?

Wake up! Call forth for a way to be shown, call for your hearts to be cleansed from hidden fears and veiled agendas.

The way to the promised land was written for all. The directions were not encoded; they were clear. There is no secrets. The way is to be found with your *own* mind and heart, not the mind and heart of another.

Do not follow without assessing who is leading. Those who followed me in my life there did so, for they thought me a fine leader. They thought me a brave and fearless way shower.

I thought that of myself until I faced my own hidden fears. Even my children, those born of my own flesh, never knew my hidden fears. If I would not take them out and look at them myself, would I show them to my children?

Truly, my intent was as pure as I could make it with my knowledge at that time but had someone questioned me and made me look at my truest motivations. would I have held up under that intensity? Would I have found the truth about myself sooner? Had someone said to me, "Martin, do you fear being less than? Do you think you are running from your own fears?" then maybe I would have stopped and remembered to delve deeper within myself.

MLK: TREATISES FROM MY LIFE

That is my point to the world: Delve deeper, burrow farther, and do not stop at the surface answers. Make those leaders accountable for their beliefs. Make them examine themselves and their teachings. If they pass the highest and most stringent of tests, then how blessed the world will become!

A great leader and a fearless way shower once said to not resist evil. *He* spoke with authority on that subject for he had a clear heart and mind. *He* knew of what he spoke. *He* understood that if you were to resist evil that you gave to it much of your power and your energy and that you were working at fearing it. *He* understood that fearing anything was a way to provide it entry to your mind and heart.

He also knew that once fear entered your heart and mind that your world would be changed. *He* knew to provide a fight against what you did not want was taking away power for you to fight for what you did want.

Fight for what you want, people, not against what you do not wish to have in your world. Make your battle cries not about the things that are wrong but about the things that need to be. Take the example of Joshua and shout out loud, not for the falling of the impeding walls but for the freedom to enter where you wish. Shout out and cry forth but do so with the things firmly in mind that you want to see come about, not what you want to eradicate. Give no resistance to evil but all your force and power to good.

In my day, there were many who fought strenuously for the eradication of war. There were those who sat in peace for peace. Had the ones who sat in peace for peace been the majority, the ways of that war would have ended sooner.

This was but another of the things that I wished I had known at that time. I joined the forces that spoke against the war. Had I been one who spoke more mightily of peace, I would have fought a better battle.

Your world now is still rocked and buffeted with war. Think before you mouth the words about not wanting war. Speak instead of the finer cause for peace. March not for peace, for marching, as I learned, often leads to more chaos, which is a form of war. Instead sit in the stillness of peace and focus upon peace. Tell your leaders how you want a peaceful world. Take no anger with you for the war, for you add the energy of anger to the war. A man who walks in peace to a peaceful thought is not one who can abide in the energy of war. Teach others by example. Be like Gandhi; sit and contemplate the desired result. Had I but truly seen the genius of Gandhi, I would have sat my butt down and taught others to see a better way.

I am trying now to teach you a better way. Resist not evil. Resist not war. Resist not learning what your inner fears are. Resist not questioning what has always been with what should be held firmly in your minds and hearts. Resist not my words today because I am long dead. Resist not the teachings of any who would hold you to a higher ideal of what man can become and who man once was.

Resistance to fear is the evil in the world today, and I have come to show that way. May your focus be on finding the truths that I found while you yet live. Do not wait, as I did, until your death to achieve such knowledge. Use that knowledge to transform that world while you are still there.

My sincerest wish is to be your way shower again and to do so with the rightness of things as they should have been when I lived. Let my voice now, though not ringing through microphones or from rafters, enter your hearts and may that be my oratory that will lead many to the promised land.

I will come again with other words, for I rest not until all can say, "Free at last, free at last. Thanks, God Almighty, I am free at last!"

Martin Luther King Jr.

The Gifts That Were Taken from Me

When I died, as I have said previously, there was a mighty fear with me. I had not realized my own depth of fear and anger until I had been shown it upon leaving that world.

I was not a man who would have thought of myself as riddled with hidden fear or tamped-down anger, but that was exactly who I was.

It was a humbling experience to come face-to-face with your own inner demons. Let me tell you!

There are no men who do not have it in them to store anger and fear. Birth into that world seems to set you up for that skill. But in this world, this world of no hidden truths and no ability to hide, you see yourself more clearly than you could even imagine.

It is a cleansing state of being, but the word *comfortable* is not the best word for this state of being either. The religious concept of eternal rest is not all wrong, for after you have corrected many things within you, there is a state of being free of those things that plague the human condition.

But let me remind you, it is not the first condition you will meet. The condition of a restful soul is earned and hard-won. It is a prize that is given only when you have completed the course.

I had reflected many times on my own shortcomings. I had reflected on the shortcomings of the movement that I led. I had reflected on the shortcomings of that world and its leaders—both in modern times and the times of my having lived there.

ROSE CAMPBELL

During all these reflections, I had come to some interesting conclusions. I had concluded that there were things taken from me—some by me and some taken from me by others. The things taken from me by me were the ones that sting the most, but I had not yet forgotten the ones taken from me by others.

If you are thinking of the world here as one of profound forgiveness, then you are not wrong.

I had seen, felt, and heard the reasons I was the victim of those things being taken from me. I had seen the greater reasons for it, and through this, I had found forgiveness for those others and even for myself.

However, I wanted to use my own example as a way to awaken you—each of you who might read these words to see that there is no surrender if you are not in accord with it from a spiritual perspective.

I had come to see the glorious perfection even in loss of things very dear to you.

When I was a man—a man with a heart that beat and a heart that loved—I knew the ills of being heartsick over things. I was often heartsick over many things. But the thing that made me most heartsick was to see my children living in fear.

I saw them huddle in fear when the crowd pressed around us. I saw them huddle in fear when the storms grew too violent— both in the sky and in the streets. I saw them huddle in fear when I exploded in my own home with rage over some slight that might have had nothing to do with them. It was I who stole much of their fearlessness, and I have had to live with that memory. I lost the joy of seeing them fearless and unknowing of fear. It was a memory I could not shake.

I also lost the faith of my wife. I was not the one who could be sure of my own faithfulness when cast out upon the road, and so I stole from myself the true depth of love that I might have had if I had been a man of more sterling character.

However, that woman who pledged her life to me was solid. She was a woman of character and strength. She loved me despite my shortcomings, and my own will to be unlovable at times. She

MLK: TREATISES FROM MY LIFE

stood beside me and mourned me when I left. She knew the pure gold of love that knew no bounds, and for this, I was in awe.

She is resting now, surer of her own soul's cleansing than I have yet been known to see. But when one is as pure as she was, the time of reflection here can be very short. She cleansed her soul in that life, and for that I was grateful. She deserved a short time of reflection here, for perfection in the body is the due of those who know true love. Hers was a rest most easily won for her role as loving wife.

I was not given to know the exact time of my death, but I did know I would be leaving that world young. The Voice had spoken to me of it. I knew that my work would culminate in my death. I knew that I would be leaving the world as a martyr, and that was my plight to carry with me day and night.

However, I did not know the time, for had I known, would I have gone from my family as often as I did? Would I have been as eager to embrace the causes of others if I knew that April 1968 was to be my last appearance to that world? I doubt I would have had the strength and courage to have done so, had I been told the exact moment of my death.

A voice telling you that you would sacrifice your life for the freedom of others was an abstract thing. It was a thing easily dismissed as a figment of your imagination. It was a nontangible thing, and one that could more easily be seen as something still coming down the road if it even appeared as was stated.

I also thought it could mean that I would be sacrificing my life in ways of not being home and not living life as most men might. But we now know that the Voice meant exactly what it said: My life was a sacrificial offering to see a work much needed gain momentum.

That is history now, friends, and of it I am not mourning. It was what was needed.

I had spoken of the most valuable things I cost myself. Oh yes, there were other much smaller things that I took from myself. There were things that would seem frivolous if I even said them on the same page as those things I had mentioned.

ROSE CAMPBELL

I will not dispense them here today, but I will now cover the things that were taken from me by others and use this as a lesson to those of you who might be losing the same things or even more pointedly to those who are taking such things from others. Pay attention. It is not an idle moment of speaking I am doing here!

I was robbed of my self-esteem when I was young. I was taught that because I was a man of color that I could not partake of the same life as those of who had less color. I was made to fear the same hands that held me—the hands that should have meant only love to me.

I lost my perspective of being valuable to society by those who saw no intrinsic value to men not born of wealth or privilege, the rights or white parents, and high scores in intelligence testing. I was made to feel less than for not having been someone seen by society at that time as having equal value. Those who had no respect to give for they themselves had not known true respect robbed me of the most basic of respect. This is a sad but true statement.

I was robbed of seeing my children grow and of knowing my part in their life. I was robbed of seeing them become parents. I was robbed of these things through a growth of fear that had infected a man who had also been robbed of these things mentioned. Those who were robbed become those who robbed. That is also a sad but true statement.

I had taken from me the joy of kissing my wife and children one more time. I was left with no further life from which to dream new dreams. I was left bleeding on a balcony and dying far from home with no family to comfort me. I was left with no friends who would walk with me as I faced the greatest trail I had yet to travel.

It was a time of great sorrow for many, but it was a time of deepest grief for me. It was I who had been robbed, and it was I who paid the price for my own part of that robbery. If you are thinking that I am waxing maudlin here, then you would be only half right.

I did regress a bit to a time that had great bearing on who I had become now in this world. But I did so with a positive focus.

MLK: TREATISES FROM MY LIFE

I did so to alert you to the ways that you robbed yourself and the ways that others could steal from you.

I also did this for you to check yourself and see if you are propagating the dastardly action of theft.

Do you treat all as you would wish to be treated? Do you steal another's self-respect to add to your own? Do you covet another's inner peace and work at undoing it even in subconscious ways? Do you steal time from another so that you can selfishly hoard time for yourself?

There are myriad ways to be a thief, my friends.

Are you aware of your part of continuing the cycle of robbery? Are you walking with the knowledge that you are giving rather than taking? Are your business transactions the ones you wish to encounter should you be on the other side of the counter? If not, then get with the rightness of being one who cares for another as you do yourself. It was a commandment of the one who came to show us the way. Have you forgotten that lesson? Do I truly need to remind you?

In any robbery, there is always a victim. However, if there is no robbery, then where do the victims go?

They, being no victim now, become the ones who can produce and be fruitful for society. Had no one robbed the victims of their pride, their respect, their joys, then how much better would the world have been at this junction in time?

These are questions that you must ponder. If you think I seek to speak of only the men of the black race, then you do me another great injustice.

Face the role of those who went before you in the robbery of the Jews, of the Native ones, of the ones who slaved for the building of many a nation, the female segment of many populations, and even the children of all nations. The list is endless, and the results are tragic.

I leave you now with much to think about. I cry not only for my own victimhood, be it from my own hand or the hand of another, but also for the victims everywhere.

Many of you who read this sermon will have been victims. Many will have been the thieves. Most will have been both at some time in their lives.

But I say to you today: The time is coming when robbery will not be tolerated. The time is coming when the act of being a thief will be seen as really having become a victim, for when you step across the divide of that life to this one, you will become the victim of your acts.

It is a truth and it is a fact. When one sets out to steal from another those things that rightfully belong to another, then the price is paid in this world.

It is also paid in that world in ways that are not so evident, but it causes a loss to society just as surely as a thief with a gun does in your home when confronting you for your valuables. The structure to society becomes unstable, and all suffer even the thieves who began the cycle. Can you not see this? Do your minds not work?

I leave you now with the knowledge that I have paid my price here. I had seen the folly of the things stolen from the ones I loved. I had seen the folly of the things taken from me and those repercussions that it created in the world. I saw still the acts of robbery, whether they be planned or by default, and I saw the suffering of all social structures due to the robberies taking place.

Walk with care and take from no man that which all men deserve. While no one loses without the spiritual will to do so, the balance of the world needs to be aligned to no one having to lose and the state of victimhood being but a sad memory. When no one loses things of great value, such as self-esteem and the right to a life lived in fulfillment of their God-given potential, then will the whole world become the winner. This I had seen.

Martin

THE RIGHT AND GLORIOUS WAYS OF LOVE

I have covered in great detail in my earlier writings about the cost and burden to the human race of fear. I have laid bare the roots of it and the ways in which it is spread one man to another.

I have pointed a signpost to the theory that will deliver the world if it is made into reality.

I wish now to lay a foundation for the argument I have to present on the grand and glorious freedom of love and the value that is taken for granted and which shall not be paid until the world sees this value.

As a man living in Georgia and other southern states, I was aware of the segregation issue of that day. I fought against it as the history books will show. However, had I been a wiser man, I would have fought instead with great zeal for the unitedness that could happen only through the use of love. I had delivered already my admittance to the right motive but the wrong devices for doing my work when I was there.

However, to sum it up for those who may not have access to those earlier writings, I will once again admit that I did not realize that by promoting the use of fear that I was engendering in the foes to my cause was actually fertilizing the spread of fear in the world. I had grabbed on to an idea of nonviolent protesting and passive resistance but did not see how eagerly I awaited the rebounding effect of fear upon those who opposed my ideologies.

This was where I erred. I used other men's fears to try and establish freedoms for the people held down with invisible bonds, and while that gave us results, it did not give the results we could have had had I used the tools of love.

The tools of love are varied and many. They are tools that are free and united—both in one action. They are tools that carve and heal—again, all-in-one swift movement. They are the metaphorical tools of a skilled surgeon working upon the diseased brains of mankind.

The tools of love do not inflict harm, and they heal both the user and the recipient of the user's intent. They are what could be termed the gifts of God to man, and they originate only in the breast of men who are attuned to the light of deity.

What are these tools? How does man purchase these tools? Are these tools for the common man with little or no knowledge of the use of them?

I can hear the thoughts of you as you read this.

My purpose in using the one who can hear my thoughts is to educate and eradicate. Let me do so.

The tools of love are, in part, the using of compassion, solidity of purpose, empathy, intelligence of mind, and control of emotion. You could also include in your metaphorical toolbox the idea of walking in another man's shoes, seeing the world through another's lenses and even hearing the sounds of another's cries were you to be placed in their position, be it financially, spiritually, or physically. It is finding a common thread of humanity despite the outward appearances of differences. It is being another man's brother.

All too often people are locked into only their own worldview and their comfort zones. How can you see the plight of your brother if you travel only down your street? How may you find the needs of another when you are so wrapped up only in the needs of self? Who can hear the sounds of another sobbing if your ears are filled only with the sounds of your own praises, often being given to you from your own ego? Where is compassion if you can turn on your televisions and see only what makes you comfortable?

MLK: TREATISES FROM MY LIFE

Where, people, are the tools you have gathered and what do you have in your toolboxes? It is time for an inventory!

I have come forward in this day and time to deliver as it was a series of sermons.

I was well-noted for my sermons while living and did not intend now to cease because some of you feel I ceased being a man of the Lord who could sermonize simply because I died.

My death was a wake-up call to me, and it had spurred me to greater levels of needing to resound the urgent callback to the ways of the Lord.

I use here words of my former livelihood since it will evoke the memory of whom I once was in those old enough to remember. But realize that my uses of those words are not limited to the frail understanding of those who have not joined me in my new form of home.

When I say the Lord, I do not mean just the Christian god. I do not mean the god of the Baptist or the Catholic or the other Christian religions. I also mean the deity of the Buddhist, Hindu, Islamic, and all who worship some form of deity.

For you see, children, there is no division! There is no god that is fragmented in such ways. There is only one deity, and despite the name you use or the understanding you have been given through religion, it is one and the same. It is the energy of love—pure and delightful love!

If God is love, as has been set forth by a Christian writer, then where my children do you think the idea of Satan comes from? If love is universal and omnipresent, what is the antithesis of love? Do I need to place another large neon signpost? Do you need to adjust your glasses? If love is the goodness of deity, then think hard. What would be the opposite of that energy? What would be the undoing of love? What is the one thing that could undo the goodness of love?

I have given you the word. I have expounded upon that word and its many manifestations. Are you thinking?

In our toolboxes that we must use to fix the world, fix the suffering, fix the broken people to end the things that break people into fractions, we must stock the tools of love. We do not have room for the tools of fear. Dump out the sludge of hate and jealousy, swab out the corners, and add to your toolbox that set of compassion and one-mindedness. Throw out greed and fill that corner of your toolbox with charity. Slide everything over and make room as well for the drill of intelligent reaction and the bits of empathy.

Let us not forget the hammer of truth either! It is a very valuable tool. Next, let us add the cloths of mercy and caring so we may cleanup the wounds we might encounter as we work.

There is much work, more work than you might imagine. Stock that toolbox well, for the project of rebuilding the world is not one of short duration. It will, however, be one that will pay exceedingly well.

Now I will address the value that is taken for granted and which the world will not understand until that value has been paid.

Can you imagine a world where no one hates another? What value is that? What about a world where children do not have to learn fear? Priceless, isn't it? What about a world where no one ever feels less than another or a man does not fear having to starve?

Yes, children, those are things of great value! Do you see that value now? Do you have that value in your pockets? No, of course not. You have long taken for granted that those things of value are not obtainable. You have taken at face value that love is not the only force in the world. But what if it is? What if the *only* force is love?

In my searches here in this place where I found myself now with no identity as a man, I had seen nothing but love. I had seen no dire consequences for those who I would have judged as sinful when I was a man preaching such jargon. I had seen no eternal damnation, a concept I had been taught to believe in while studying in my schools of theology. I had seen no form of evil or wickedness, which you would expect to find since many whom I had encountered here were once men or women upon your planet.

In truth, all I had found was love. Love radiated as the rays of the sun here; it was all pervasive. There was no feeling of evil nor of fear.

I did now believe that was fully a man-made structure, and it was the source of the problems plaguing the world you live in.

I had come to see that love was the full truth of heaven and that there was no need to fear the other alternative that many would have you believe in. How sorely I was grieved that I once taught such a fearful concept!

Had I been a perfect man—a man with no flaws of my own, I would have expected this sort of heaven. But I was not a perfect man. History and biographies had recorded my flaws and my vices.

I was a man, simple as that, with the failings and malfunctions that all men may be prone to. I was not a man who could have been held up as perfect, and that was apparent. I had vanity, I had weaknesses, I had the belief that I was profoundly right in my course of action. This I had proven to myself as a wrongful thing and had shared that insight with you through these writings.

No, children, I was not a man who should have seen a heaven of such perfection.

While my actions were indeed less in nature of wrongfulness than those of others, I would never say that I deserved the love I had found, but this was what I have seen—a love so profound and all-encompassing as to make you weep. It filled me, lifted me, and radiated through me and out of me. It was the *only* thing here in heaven.

It was the God I thought I knew when I called his name and preached his name even in my flawed conceptions of him. Even my conceptions of him as a him were wrong.

The real state of God is total love. That man who penned those words who found their way into the Christian Bible was indeed correct: God is love.

Let me be a witness to that man's writings. Let me be the one to tell you now that truer words have never been written.

If I had found heaven, which in me there was no doubt, then how could any man who lived and had his heart with God be anything but eager to experience and propagate the experience of love?

God is but a name, as is Allah and the other words used to define deity.

Deity is love. It matters not what you have been taught by men who focus on former teachings. It matters not what you call this concept.

The truth is that there is *only* love, and love is what we all seek. Your world is driven to many things in the name of seeking love.

But think on this: If there is not love being used to find love, how can you ever expect to know love? The wars in the name of Allah or of God, the hoarding of possessions and imbalance of daily sustenance to every person on earth, the use of force to hold others down, and the need for one group to feel superior, are these experiences of love? Are these reflections of love? Does love beget these things?

How can a man, any man, feel right within himself if they are seeking to be one with their deity if they are not reflecting the powers of that deity? How can they hope to be granted the internal experience of deity if they are aligned with those things that are counter to the experience of that deity?

All things that do not use the tools of love are as the chaff that will be revealed to be useless. It will be the undoing of that world if the tools of love are not used to rebuild it.

I speak now with vehemence and righteous volume for the understanding of what is truth. I am crying out from my heaven to your world to make clear the misconceptions that I myself once believed.

There is no greater glory than love. Love is the experience of deity, for deity is love.

That is my great revelation to you. It is my penance for correction of my own part in not understanding and leading others as I should have when I was among you.

Listen to my voice as those who did then. I have indeed now seen the promised land, and it is a land of love, only love.

MLK: TREATISES FROM MY LIFE

Let fear be no more, let fear mislead you no more, let fear be seen and exposed as the thing that separates men from deity!

All I offer to you is sent with love. It is given because of love. I am led by love. No more does fear reside in me, and this is the most glorious and fulfilling state of existence.

There is no will to be any other way. The plight of men is the introduction of fear to their minds and hearts. When the fear is spread through the false ideas of religion, education, and nationalism, there is a moving away from deity.

See those flaws! See the misuse of intellect and power being given to you. See the truth, children, for the truth shall set you free. Those are the second greatest words ever written, and I bear witness to those words as well.

I am the essence of a man who once led with great love of freedom for many, but had I led with only love, then how much better the march would have been to that promised land?

See the glory as I am revealing it to you. I do not express any of these truths solely of my own accord, for I am directed by love to do so.

I am not the only one who has given these revelations. I follow in the wake of other men who saw the truth and were led by love to declare the glory of it. My blessing has been to return and find one who could repeat my words and reveal these truths to set the record straight. Listen as you have not listened in the past.

The time to use the tools of love is now, and work done with these tools will produce a return of the freedom of all men to know love as it exists in heaven.

Give your children that gift that they may not know the fears you have known and that they may teach their children only with the tools of love. Build homes using these tools. Erect schools with these tools that teach these tools. Worship with love to bring love to your worship. Define no country with borders that have not been built with tools of love and watch as men from every nation begin to work with love. Let neither man nor woman ever again feel that love is missing for in truth there is naught but love.

ROSE CAMPBELL

The darkness of fear must flee in the light of love. When the world sees only the light of love, fear will cease to even be remembered except in history books and even then it shall be seen as a lesson, not a state of desired existence.

I leave you with love and know that I exist in love and that all exist in love if they can see through the false fears handed to them. Praise be the truth!

Martin Luther King Jr., a man who once lived in fear and who now resides in love.

THE GLORIOUS USE OF WILL

O ne of the things I have learned here in this place is that what I wish comes to be with amazing speed. If I set my will to be in Chattanooga, then I am transported to the memories I have of that place with no hesitancy. It is almost like that old tale of the genie who grants every wish.

It is amazing and somewhat difficult to get accustomed to. I have found myself wishing I had not wished some things.

However, as with being in your world, there is a time of adjustment needed for any newly learned skill. I have now mastered the art of getting around with no unpleasant detours.

The use of one's will here is speedy, ever-changing, and dependent upon the amount of wish fulfillment you use. I can think thoughts and not be removed from where I reside in the twinkling of an eye. Don't think that I am being transported willy-nilly by every random thought. It is not at all like that. However, if I think of something with great yearning or eagerness, then I am often found in that environment.

I once wished I could review my life in jail to see how that impacted my further decisions upon being released. It was indeed a learning experience to reexperience that particular memory and to feel the shifting fluids of emotion again. I did not spend great amounts of time wishing I could stay in that space, believe me.

I was not aware when I was living as a man that my thoughts had a great deal of bearing on my shifting world back then. Yes, I knew I thought of things, and then they happened, but did I see the correlation? Not entirely.

I, like most of you, just thought it was the standard flow of life to think of things and have a certain amount of those things come around to your life. I never caught that sometimes the very thing I wished for came to be. This was, to a great degree, because I was very busy almost every moment of every day.

But it was also because the speed with which things were given due to thought was much delayed in your world. Most often by the time I got what I had been thinking, I had forgotten I had thought that exact thought. Only in hindsight did I ever catch that what just happened or what I just received was something I had been thinking.

Due to my busy life, however, I didn't spend much time on hindsight in trivial matters. I missed so much of the small miracles that I had received.

Is that happening to you? Are you too busy to catch the times that the very thing you thought of and wished for, even in a subconscious manner, was delivered to your very doorstep? Do you ever review your thoughts when something happens that shouldn't have and see the links between your earlier thoughts and the thing you just witnessed or received? Do you remember such instances when something you thought about came into being and you caught that? If not, then don't waste your life being unaware!

Pay attention, children! You are receiving just as I did, just as all were. Here it is a much shorter time between wish and wish fulfillment. It is easier to make the connection—both in the receiving of the thing wished for and in the seeing of how the wish came to be. In the world you live in, it often takes some time, perhaps even years, for that wish to be fulfilled. Why is that?

The secret is not the things wished for. It is not the number of times you wish for something. It is not the gift of being special or closer to God to receive miracles.

No, children, it has nothing to do with your special status with the deity that many call God. It has to do only with your own emotional makeup and emotional powers. It is the amount of power in your emotional connection with the wish that makes it a speedy or delayed event.

MLK: TREATISES FROM MY LIFE

Thinking a random thought was not power enough to create the thing you thought of. If that was the case, then your world would be besieged with far too many things and things really not wanted. The power of thought was a fine tool, but it was not *the* tool used to create and manifest things in your experience. It was the tool used first to get the job started, but to refine that job, you must use a far more special tool: the tool of emotional energy.

When I was in the position of being jailed, there was a great amount of emotion involved as you can well imagine. It was not a hard thing to generate the amount of emotion that it took to create something, for it was an emotional experience. It was a time of great power for me, though I did not realize it at the time you see.

One of the pieces of literature that is ascribe to me and known as one of my finer works by some was a letter I had written from jail. It was indeed a good letter if I must say so myself.

However, do you think that the power of that letter came through solely of my own devices? Do you think that the words alone would have been enough to have been sufficient if I had not been emotionally involved in that piece of writing?

Hardly. Had I written that letter sitting at my desk with the love of family readily available to me, the freedom to walk out and be in the world readily available to me or the knowledge that I would be able to sleep with my wife that night granted to me with no restrictions, the tone would have been different.

Would that letter have contained the same emotion generated as when these things were denied to me? Never. It was the emotion that brought forth that letter, the impact it had, and the changes it wrought.

The thought to write the letter had been on my mind prior to that confinement in jail. Some of the key points in that letter were ever-present in my mind prior to that lockup. But I swear to you that it was the emotional framework that I found myself in that gave rise to that particular letter written exactly as it was.

I had wished to write a letter when I was a freeman to open the eyes of more people. I had wished to address some issues. However, if I had written it without the emotion contained within it, the effect would have been muted for my input would have been muted. I was the author only in thought, but the power lay in a higher realm. It lay in the realm of pure emotion.

My point here by regressing to a point in my earthly life is this: When you put great emotion behind an otherwise random thought, it is coming more powerfully and more swiftly than you can imagine. If you think only a random thought with no emotional fuel, then it might be never that the thing thought of arrives.

It is not the thought, folks; it is the emotion that makes it viable in your world. The stronger the emotion, the more power of manifestation it had in your world.

The barriers to arrival are stronger on your world and for good reason. Most of you are not cognizant of the power you hold. If you live as I do now in this place, you will not be able to function with all that would be changing in your world with the mere thought of something making it appear. Your state of confusion would be mind-bending. But if you are unsure of what I say, think of this: Do not miracles most often happen in your world when there is a dire emergency? When someone is hurt or dying, things are at a loss? Why is this? What do you suppose? Could it be that the emotional foundations of those times are greater, and anything thought of this time would have more power? Does the seed of emotion stay the same when you are in crisis versus when your life is good? Of course not! The power of miracles arises from that heightened emotional power. It is the way of creating.

I bring this reminder to you now because your world needs to know that the use of miracles is not a fallacy. It is not the spinning of tales. There are indeed miracles happening every day—both large and small. Some are obvious, some are not. Only the awakened to their place in the power structure of the world as a place of energy seem to catch the smaller ones. However, many of you, once your eyes are opened to the fact of miracles, the reason and the cause of miracles will begin to see for yourselves.

I do not ask you to believe out of hand. Pay attention, be diligent with your thoughts, and remember that emotion is the real juice to the drink of having what you wish.

MLK: TREATISES FROM MY LIFE

There is no straw that interferes with you drinking from this mixture except your disbelief and your unawareness of the nature of miracles. It is a full cup; all may drink, and it ever replenishes itself. Do not sit and cry because you are thirsty!

I close now with this rejoinder: All that you will must be if you are emotionally connected to it. It is a given here and could be for you as well.

There are no barriers except the ones you have erected, and no one may remove those except yourself.

It may not be immediate as it is in my experience, but the greater the emotion, the more swift the arrival.

Use the gift of the barriers to immediate reception of what is willed to hone your truest wishes. And as the old saying goes, please do be careful of what you wish for!

Wishing you opened eyes,

Martin

THE CONSENSUS OF CONSCIOUSNESS

In my earlier writings, I had addressed the subject of fear, its manipulations of mankind, and the purveyors of that fear. I had addressed a few ways to redefine the thoughts of men and the tools to use for a reformation of the current state of affairs.

Let me now tell you of the vast pool that resides here in this land of my abode from which I speak.

There were many things that were difficult to convey from this world to that one. Had I been privy to a glimpse of it in my life there as Martin Luther King, I would have been woefully inadequate at understanding it and relaying it using only the words I knew.

Bear in mind that I had a good command of language and the art of speaking, but I know I would have been hard-pressed to begin the description of what actually exists here.

Such is my plight even now. The one I am using as a typist was also one who had a better than basic vocabulary and an art of conveying ideas, but my words to you through her were still going to be expressed in shortness of the truth of what existed here.

But my attempt might prove to be adequate enough if you allow the words to form a bridge between what you read and what you feel. In that place, you may be able to understand with knowledge greater than mere words could impart.

There existed a vast pool. It was not a pool of water or even of air. It was a pool of intelligence as it was. It was the pool of all

MLK: TREATISES FROM MY LIFE

that mankind had known and was right now formulating in their consciousnesses. It swirled and had great energy.

There existed an effervescence about it. It eddied and flowed just as an ocean does. It was never stagnant and was ever-refreshed.

There was a sound to it of a multitude of whispers. It was the collective mind of all who had awareness even down to the animals. While it would be easy to think that this pool could be called God, I was of the understanding it was not, at least in the fullness of what God would be.

When I was allowed to see this pool, I wanted to fall to my proverbial knees—such was the feeling of awe that I had.

I now do believe that many of the writers who penned many of the descriptions of mysterious things in the writings—such as the Bible, Koran, and the Torah—were men, who, while living, had seen the edges of this pool. I can certainly understand they're trying to convey the experience and the difficulty that they might have had.

I was shown this pool by those who had taken me to task for some of my former thinking. They brought me to the edge of the pool, though I was not allowed to see directly into the midst of it. I was not allowed to experience a mingling with that pool, though I wanted badly to see what the experience would be like.

How can I describe the oddity of understanding that while I stood at the brink of this pool, I knew that even my thoughts of the pool were being added to it?

My tour guides made this fact clear to me. I could feel the pull of it even into my own mind, for the energy and power of it is all-invasive when within its presence. The yearning to meld into it was all alluring.

I was removed from its presence, but the feeling of it in my own mind did not diminish. With great and startling clarity, I suddenly understood something. I understood that the feeling was not new and that just being at the pool's edge did not bring it on.

What had been ever there had been made aware to me. In simpler terms, I understood that I had just been shown what was always there, but I had been unaware of it since I had grown so used to it. But the journey to the pool's edge had awakened my awareness to that pull, that yearning for connection to it.

It was what had been there driving me on as a man, what had been my ever-present urge to see that things were a righted in men's minds at my time of life there in your world. It was the force that drove me.

Having already disclosed the flaw in myself and my work while there due to hidden fear, I will not transgress into another sermon on that subject but will mention it briefly to make a point here for why I have chosen to speak now on the pool of consciousness. My driving force for good was the pull of that pool.

I wanted to add something of good to that pool. I wanted to make a contribution that would infuse the pool with better thoughts, a better form of energy.

I was working to make an eddy within it that stood for something higher and more righteous that I had seen around me in my life there as a man. No, I was not aware of this, but that became clear to me as I left the presence of the pool, and I do believe that was why I was taken to the edge of it. I was taken there to show me the impetus of my earthly life I had left.

However, when I became aware of that, I also became more fully aware of the fact that my hidden fear and its agenda had convoluted that impetus. It had warped the truest intent I had on a subconscious level, and to my great consternation, I realized that I had also added to the pool eddies of fear. Not my own, for they had already existed.

I had stirred up and promoted the growth of fears of other men. I had raised the decibels of fear among those I had been challenging. Yes, I had added good with the raising of awareness of the need for freedom and equality for all but had also sent packets of fear and hate spinning off into that pool. How great that consternation was when I realized what I had done!

As I said earlier in my discourses, there was no judgment here, no dire consequences from that what most would call God. All my instructions and revelations were given to me with the feeling of great love. Never have I felt the sting of reproach.

MLK: TREATISES FROM MY LIFE

However, the process does indeed make you see and understand with a clarity that you cannot have when you are limited by a man's mind and man's physical processes. The only judgment I had had was my own upon myself, and truly, this was quite sufficient to make one want to weep!

The bout of clarity that came to me from my time at the pool's edge was force enough to make me determined to return using another to relay my words to you. I came again to deliver the knowledge that while there is no judgment upon your actions while there and therefore also your soul except yourself, as far as I have determined, that alone is enough to bring you to your knees, figuratively speaking here. There is no one to cause you to bow your head in shame except yourself. But trust me in this: The act of being forced to bow your head in shame by your own acknowledgment is indeed a dire consequence if your actions warrant it.

The pool, which is the consensus of consciousness, was a great motivator and a great leveler. I had no knowledge if all were taken to the pool, though my feeling was indeed a place many visit in their time of instruction. But it mattered not if you would visit it as I did or not. It existed, and the power in that statement was this: Every thought and therefore every deed you do and do not do are flowing in that pool.

The thoughts you have while reading my words, whether they are for or against what I say, are added. The thoughts you think in private, which are never expressed to another living being, are added. The thoughts you entertain, the thoughts you do not even consciously catch yourself thinking, are added. Do you see what I am saying? Do you understand the real reason I am here telling you this?

I was given to understand that the flow of this pool, the pull of it was a two-way mechanism. All that was thought was pulled to the pool. Every mind was connected to that pool, and all thoughts from every mind fed the pool.

However, just as all minds fed the pool, all minds may feed from the pool. It was a fountain of knowledge and may well have been the genesis of the tree of knowledge of good and bad, written about in Genesis. (Yes, wit does still reside in me!)

If that should be a truth, think on this: All that you add is being made available to all others. It is the way in which those who have extended spiritual gifts may know of the thoughts and conditions of another.

It is the reason Jesus could easily fathom the truth of the minds of those he encountered. It is how mystics can possess knowledge that does not reside within their own personal knowing. There are greater mysteries that exist than these, dear children!

Now if that indeed be the case, what is it you are feeding into the pool? Can you see how your thoughts could be creating the world you see? If you think on the dark, the fearful and the forbidden, then you add eddies of that to the pool.

Another who can, even without awareness of it, make a connection to those eddies and may well be pulling on that which you have added! They may be acting upon that which you did not but which you added to the pool of consciousness by your power of thought.

Conversely, if you train the mind to dwell on the better, the higher, the greater of thoughts, then where are the connections to the dark and despairing acts?

They are buried under the layers of the positive and constructive ideas. Access to them is harder to reach. Do you get it now? Do you see? Can you hear me?

I am not confessing that I know the greatest of truths. No, I am well-aware that I am not of that magnitude as of yet. However, I have been given some clarity of my own acts and my own thoughts while I was a man where you are now.

I have been made aware that I added to the pool a layer of good, uplifting ideas and actions. But I am also aware that I added a layer or more of fear and anger. I despair that those layers might be feeding those who wish to feed off of anger, hate, fear, and destruction.

I pray that my good layers are feeding those who also wish to see the good things for mankind. But I come to you to instruct

MLK: TREATISES FROM MY LIFE

what I was given; the knowledge that what we add is not only merely added but also drawn upon.

Let your reading of my words to you through my secretary be a lesson. Let yourself monitor your thoughts and remember that you feed the greater multitudes through this pool. Just as the man known as Jesus fed the multitudes with a little bit, you do so as well. Focus the power of your thoughts to the highest level. Focus the deeds you do from those thoughts and let them be as a blessing to those you encounter.

All are added to the pool. Remember this, remember it well. May you never have to bow your head in shame for what you have added to the pool called consciousness from this time forward. I wish for you what I myself have endeavored to attain.

Martin

The Seeds that Fell upon Rocky Soil

I have mentioned in my last writings the gifts of hearing and seeing the realms of heaven, but if you feel that is the entire list of gifts given to mankind from the spiritual source of our beginning, then you are not thinking again! Why would the source of all understanding give gifts that needed an equivalent in the physical bodies that were made? Would it not be wiser to also imbue the new beings with what always existed? Why gift these new creatures with anything less than they had been in the spiritual realms? Why deny them any access to your voice? It doesn't hold water, does it, children?

In these spiritual realms where I now move freely, I am not a body. I am a mind. I do not have eyes, and yet I see. I have no ears, and yet I hear. I have no skin, and yet I feel. I possess a way of knowing things that have no grounding in anything reminiscent to my former body as Martin Luther King.

Yes, I remember that body and that man. I remember the highlights of that life led as that being. But surely I tell you: I am much more than that. I am more than I ever knew when I lived as that man. I do not think and will even say with certainty that I am not special. Each of you are more than you can know while you live there as men and women.

If you wish to speak of odd things, ponder upon meeting the true aspect of someone you loved when living as a man.

MLK: TREATISES FROM MY LIFE

I had met the soul who had been my wife Coretta. Yes, we instantly knew each other, though we did not reside in those same bodies.

Our remembering of each other had nothing to do with those physical bodies. It was the soul of each of us that drew us together when we lived in bodies, and it was the soul of us that remembers those ties. The reunion was not one of flesh meeting flesh but rather of our minds again drawn together into a blissful rejoining.

I again am at a loss of words to fully convey to you the quality and rapture of that experience. But it confirmed to me that what we were in that world did not leave us when we died. It was a blessing, for the recognition of each other in this life was valuable for many reasons. I will clarify that statement in a moment.

Having again been joined with one who played an important role in my life as Martin the preacher man and as Martin the civil rights worker was like instantly knowing why I had come there to be those things. I could instantly feel and see and hear myself from her perspective of me. Once the minds join in this realm, there was very little hidden. It brought clarity to each of us when we joined with those who also joined us in earthly life.

I could not stress to you strongly enough to be aware of how you interact with every person you share a life with. Remember my words about there being no judgment here other than your own as you remember that former life? I shared with you how it was to have your own head bowed in shame by your own acknowledgments of your former deeds and the reasoning for them.

That was but a partial truth of those things you will encounter in your time here in the realm of heaven. Imagine meeting a loved one from that same life as a man or woman and fully seeing, fully knowing what they saw of you, saw in you, and how they viewed you. It was a moment of intense self-awareness and judgment of yourself.

Be kind to one another so that your time of meeting with them here will not be a moment of intense sorrow and shame.

To return to my topic of the gifts that were given, think about these things: Have you ever felt the presence of someone

75

before you saw them? Have you ever known something that you were stymied about as to how you knew that it would come to be? How about knowing, with no objective reason, what someone was going to say or do before the event happened? Have you ever had a dream that came true or played out in front of you? Oh yes, and what about those moments of déjà vu that you have witnessed? These were the things I was here to remind you of today.

I had entitled this sermon "The Seeds That Fell Upon Rocky Soil" for a purpose. I had established for you a partial list of those things that mankind possesses that they do not readily use and often do not give credence to.

The depth of that list was never ending, but I had mentioned the more prevalent of the ones noted by most.

All possessed these things; it was just that many were not aware of their daily thoughts and urges. These were the ones who slumber most deeply.

My title did derive from a biblical parable, for I was once a teacher of that book and am well-versed in that vein. However, I used this not only for that fact that it came from the Bible but also as a means of tying in my urge to have been a sower of peaceful and verdant equality among men from that former life time.

The parable was one of men sowing seeds into a field. Some of the seeds landed on good soil. They sprouted and produced a ripe yield. However, some seeds were wasted, for they fell upon rocky soil and were dried by the sun and eaten by the birds. Their potential came to naught. Can you guess how this parable might tie in with my topic of today? Are you getting a tingle about what I am about to say?

The latent gifts that human fleshly men possess were given to all. Those gifts were spread out equally. None was left. The fields of human experience were not left barren and destitute. The potential for a ripe yield of spirit within flesh was sown. Not one field was without the potential for growth and harvest. However, using my clever analogy a bit further, some of the fields were more fertile, more ready for sprouting, and production of yield.

MLK: TREATISES FROM MY LIFE

Others, being a bit rockier by nature, were not fields that were conducive to taking the seeds sown and propagating the potential found there. The seeds sown lay barren and tossed aside, thrown as it was to the hot sun of denial and the birds of disbelief.

The seeds were the ties to the realms of heaven. The fields were each one of you who exist in physical bodies as a man or a woman.

The yield of the seeds was a firmer connection with the true source of your being. The sun of denial and the birds of disbelief were self-explanatory. Many of you basked in that sun and fed those birds.

Your seeds were being wasted; they produced naught. Your lives were less verdant, and your yield of spiritual connection was withering away. Each passing generation that your fields laid dormant, the rockier they became. Do you get what I am saying? Do you have ears to hear?

The rocks found in the field of human experience were the same as those monsters under your bed that I spoke of before. Each fear you harbored, each time you turned from things not proven by your sciences, each day that you did not seek the Voice, you became rockier. Your soil became less viable for the implantation of those seeds given to all men. You became as the fields that lay fallow and did not produce, denying all the bounty of what you could have given. Is this the legacy you wish leaving for your children and your children's children?

Spiritual starvation did exist as surely as physical starvation. Did you feed, or did you deny? Did you add onto, and did you feed the multitudes with what you could?

The seeds of knowing the thoughts of others had been sown—the seeds of knowing the thoughts of angels, and I used this term to mean all who live in the spiritual realms, had been sown.

The seeds of having prior knowledge of things to come were strewn over your fields of experience. The seeds of vision and prophecy were sown as recorded in those books of religion.

77

ROSE CAMPBELL

Do not waste those seeds! Do not deny those seeds! To do so makes you less of a man living a coexistence with spirit.

Spirit was your truest nature. Why deny your connection to it as you walk as a man? Toss those rocks out of your field. Clear the way for a productive yield as you till your gardens of life. Learn what I wish I had known. Be as I should have been!

My sermons were meant to awaken. They were meant to create a remembrance. They did not chastise needlessly.

I would not spare the time from my state of being here or ask that time be given from the woman who types my words if I did not see the need. The time had long since passed that I, as a man, led fleshly people toward a better world.

But my purpose had not changed. Each and every word I have written was meant to still lead souls to a fuller understanding of heaven and each other. I had taken what I was as a man and added to it what I now know and am giving you the things that I wished I had awakened to when I was just such a man.

The time to wake up and see, really see the fullness of the human experience, as it was meant to be, was now at hand. Do not slumber any longer. The world needed those who were arising. It needed those who could produce more using the seeds given.

The plight of spiritual starvation was evident! Feed your own lives, and by doing so, you fed the lives of those around you.

Every man was a gift, and every man had a gift. Let not your seeds dry upon rocky soil!

Farmer Martin

THE UNITED FORCES OF AMERICA

There would be no man who could assume to be prouder of his country than I was.

I was, in my own mind, a fine citizen of my country of birth, and I took great pride in the strides of that country for freedom of thought and expression for the majority of men.

However, as history will bear out, I was not as enamored of it for the freedom of expression that was given to many in my time.

Having said that, it bore witness to the greatness of my country of birth as the man known as Martin Luther King Jr. that I was allowed to present my disquiet and unrest with the status quo. Yes, surely.

I was jailed but not for the idea of protesting but rather for the idea that I had to do so within certain bounds set by men who had not taken the spirit of the laws into full account. I was not jailed because I protested in theory but rather for protesting as I did. I brought much of that jail time upon myself for pushing the envelope of resistance and for the art of bringing attention to my cause. Thus, I still asserted that the gift of the right to protest was mine and that of all men in that country.

The force that was America is a fine example of how theory and reality do not often coexist. Lest anyone think I was about to embark upon a diatribe against my former country, let me clarify that statement. I was not jailed because I dared to speak my mind. The Lord knew I spoke loudly with conviction. The folks who heard me knew I was fired up about my causes. I was jailed

ROSE CAMPBELL

because all men did not embrace the theory of freedom of expression as a reality.

It was not the fault of the country as much as it was the fault of the few. The ideal that built America held its power and its genius despite the failings of the few to adopt the truest meaning of that platform. The theory was sound; the reality was still in its throes of being birthed.

I had the ear and the interest of many great men. I had the backing and the financial support of many who stood for that theory. I marched with many who also stood for that principle. I marched against many who also understood and adopted that principle.

However, the convictions of some were not fully anchored in that resounding principle with the trueness of its full intent. History will show though that even those who would have convoluted the meaning to fit their narrower adaptation of it did so with full conviction as well.

Herein lies my thesis that the forces of America must be joined in its efforts to adopt, down to the roots of all men, the great and abiding spirit of the laws that the country was founded upon.

The ideal of freedom for all men was something that was easy to say and to write but another matter entirely to live. The idea that all had equal say and power to express their firmly held beliefs, be they religious or personal, was something that took much striving to embrace in the fullness of that statement.

My work was not to undo the freedoms of others when those freedoms were based upon the ideals of that country but rather to enrich those ideals. How could I adopt the ideals of my country and live there in pride if I saw great injustices being done to the foundation of that country? History will show I could not.

In that country today, there are many who would espouse the same ideology of the founding fathers, and yet they, like the men I encountered, would do so only if it did not interfere with their projected way of living.

I ran afoul of those who wanted the American freedom, the American ideals in their lives, but were unwilling to see that it

MLK: TREATISES FROM MY LIFE

needed to be for all men, not just those of certain socioeconomic or racial backgrounds. To ensure those very same things for only one segment or one arena of the population was to make a mockery of the American ideal. That mockery still exists and still needs to be brought to light.

I once said that to walk as a man who carried a heavy burden was to be a man who had no hope. If there was within America segments of the population who feel they had no hope, then had we come far enough as a species to warrant pride? Had we truly walked enough miles to follow in the footsteps of the great men who saw a better way for human life? Would we find ourselves an enriched world or a world only repeating the same mistakes that we craved to leave in our forefather's day? What about the world as a whole? Could we say that we were a beacon of righteousness to the others who had yet adopted an ideal of freedom for men?

I speak metaphorically here for I was no longer a man to be counted as an American, but I was a soul who could be counted as still striving for the greatness of that American dream.

It was a dream that could be applied in theory to the world if the forces of America took that dream to heart and took it to the world as an example. It was a theory that might become a reality in the world if America could make it a reality that showed itself viable.

This was my reason for again speaking as a man who once lived in the pursuit of that dream.

I had outlined in a former statement of mine how I was able to come forth now and speak as I once did. There was no magic to it; there was no miracle involved.

I was a man who always found ways to make my presence known, and I was no less that force now. I had been in contact with the woman who took my words to paper for several years now. She had only now begun to allow me the freedom to speak as I wish and to record my words.

I did not mean to disparage her for not allowing me to do so before this time because in truth, I had to wait until the time was right for us both and for the introduction again of my voice to that world.

To make short shift of this topic, let me say this: I was not an orator for my own purposes. I was an orator for the purposes of a greater cause. I firmly believed that then and knew it now to be a truth. I was born in that world to be a leader for the beginning of a work that I carry on even now.

I will not be silent as long as injustice still plagues mankind, and I am making use of a woman who can hear my thoughts to record even now my work for the cause of setting to rights the things that need attention.

She is not of my mindset; she is not of my convictions in the most far reaching of ways. She has not walked the paths I have walked, but she is a woman who will record with great clarity and nonbias the things that I said.

Upon our introduction many years ago, she was found to be uneducated in my life's history. She found that a lacking on her part and did investigate some of who I was.

However, her part in this was solely as a secretary. Her knowledge of my former life was not an issue here. However, I was glad to be working with one who cared enough to see who I had been. But that did not equate to knowing who I am now.

I was using her, and in this, she was not to be blamed. My words were my own; my remonstrative tone was my own. My indignation and power of conviction was my own. Do not doubt that I carried with me to this new place much of what I was there, and do not cast an eye of contempt upon the one who brings you my words. I was and am still my own man if that term may be used in this case.

Now let me continue with my treatise.

The power that once was given to the men who founded that country had not diminished. Do you not see that the will of those men to create a strong and viable refuge for those who did not wish to be confined to prescribed religious and military control was God-given? Has not the ideals of those times held great beckoning power to many around the world? Will America have

MLK: TREATISES FROM MY LIFE

grown to the power structure it is without the world recognizing the greatness behind its foundation? In less time than most countries had ever been built, America had risen to a power that made it a superstructure that others depend upon. It had shown the way to greater wealth, greater advancements, and greater ideas than the founders could have envisioned. It had grown, for the foundations laid were solid and blessed.

Let me say here that if anyone begins to think that I am partial to America over the other lands of the world, then they are missing the greater intent of my message.

I am not partial to America for her land, her citizenry, her wealth, and her place in the world market. I am partial to the ideal that America was built upon. It was an ideal that would serve the entire world well, but only if the American people could make it a reality.

This is my message. This is my calling for you today. However, I speak not only to the American people. I speak to the men of all nations. Look at the pretext of what is the theory that became America. Look at the intent of that foundation. Hear what was not written in the words adopted as that nation's tenet of power. Look harder at the spirit and the will behind those pieces of paper!

The will of America to be what was envisioned does reign in most of its citizenry. The will of most of the people who were adopted into that country is to become one with that ideal. The world looks at the facts as presented by the American people and judges the ideal.

Do you not see, my fellow world citizens, that an ideal of this nature is meant not for only one country but for the world as a whole? Had I been born in any other country, I am assured that I would have looked to the ideal that is the American foundation and fought to bring it to my own land.

It was not an ideal that had any certain flag to claim, it was an ideal that may claim all flags if the will of the people of those lands were to recognize the genius of the spirit behind it.

Let no man think me biased; I am a citizen of no country now, and yet I come forth to discourse upon the theoretical foun-

ROSE CAMPBELL

dations of that particular country. Why? Is it because I was born to that country in my last life as a man? No, for I had been in many countries during my life there and saw many good people from all countries. Is it because I want to disenfranchise those other countries? Never! I am coming forth now and am speaking for this way of thinking because I had been made aware of the truth of its underpinnings and its origins. I had seen the hand that wrote the words, and it was not the hands of the men ascribed as authors.

America was the aegis of a new order, a new way of men living in peace and fulfillment. It was given as a sign of the times to come, and if that sounds cryptic, then let me clarify: There was no reign that would begin in heaven until such time as the reality of the theory that became the American constitution was adopted by all lands and all creeds. It was the blueprint given by the Lord himself, and I call now for the American people, all people, to begin to bring that theory to reality!

If you think me possessed, consider the story of my life while I was there. Was I not possessed then of a desire to find justice and freedom for those who had been held down by a breach of applying the fullness of the spirit of those laws? Was I not a man possessed of the need to see that all men and women were treated as equal, had the right to speak, worship, and learn as all others had the right?

My zeal today is not different than my zeal then; I had but a better understanding of the reasons of my zeal then and now. I was a man of the Lord then and am a man of the Lord even now. I had been shown the fullness of that theory and the things brought up out of it if it ever reaches the height of what the true Author intended when he gave it to be written by men's hands.

Listen well now, children, it isn't my own voice crying out; it isn't my own agenda that I proclaim. I have been lead and blessed to speak these words, and I do so with the same zeal as I did when I led the marches, led the masses to see a better way.

Defy not my words, for they are not mine. The words penned two hundred plus years ago were not the words of mere man. Do you not see this? Do you not feel this?

MLK: TREATISES FROM MY LIFE

I had for a time when living there considered living abroad. That was not a well-known fact.

Coretta and I had discussed this. But we felt that our fight was not for other countries, for other lands. We considered living abroad for the safety of our children. We considered this for the peace it would ensure them.

However, we knew that the work I was doing would be diluted if we left America and ventured our family life in other directions. It would not have had the impact that it did had I left and resided in any other country. Why? Because we knew that only in that country, with its constitutional rights, we could fully make the statement that needed to be made. Had we moved the children and our home to another land, then my work would have been less meaningful.

I had to fight where I lived, and I had to live where I fought. While it would have accorded my family a more serene existence, it would not have been the right thing to do to show the world that I wanted freedom for America's repressed if I tucked my family away in another country.

We were Americans, and that was what gave us the right to protest the treatment of others that would one day affect our own children. Think on this then: If I could not leave my family and they could not live as was intended by the founders of the country, then why would I not march even harder to see the fruits of that theory become reality? Why are you not marching to ensure the same thing for your children and their children?

I speak here not to the black families alone. Yes, there is still much road to travel for those who want equality, but the fight is not any longer about black versus white, poor versus rich, or any other thing that was my platform when I was there. It is now about bringing a new blueprint to completion and seeing the house that could be built if everyone worked upon it.

Do not let the boundaries of race, economic status, religion, or nationalism be boundaries any longer. See humanity as a family and a family that needs family counseling.

Yes, I said counseling. Would you treat another the same as yourself if you thought them a brother or a sister? Would you snatch away the lands of your brother or speak ill of your sister if you had the right mindset? If you cannot see those who bear a different color of face or has less jingle in their pockets as a sibling, then that is why I suggest counseling.

Families in crisis need counseling. It was part of my work as a minister. The family of the human race is in crisis; it has been for far too long.

Let the word *counseling* be a hint. Let the idea of working with your *siblings* in constructive ways be a goal.

Would I come forth and speak on the structure of one country over another when it matters not since I reside no longer in any country if I had not seen a better way? Would I take the lead in something that I had not felt was worth the fight?

The things I had seen were well worth the effort. The things I had seen were priceless, and the cost of changing yourselves was not too dear! Notice please I say changing yourselves. You cannot change one other person, and that is a valuable hint as well.

The force of war is the act of trying to change another into believing and behaving as you would wish them too. However, if people could change themselves to align with the ideals as set forth in that glorious tenet that built America, then the force of wars and strife would soon be forgotten.

In my previous dissertation to my typist, I discussed the effects of fear upon men.

Those words hold true to this treatise as well. If a man harbors fear in his heart, then what is the result? He becomes a bearer of the things that create war and strife.

Therefore, I might suggest that each of you begin to find and evaluate the fear deep within you. Do you fear being recognized as less than your *siblings*? Do you fear them taking from you those things that do not matter in the end of your life anyway? Do you fear being not valued and loved? What are your fears, children? How do they affect your ability to make equality a reality for all men? How do they affect your relationship with all other humans?

MLK: TREATISES FROM MY LIFE

Are they valid fears or did others who feared hand them to you and you accepted them without knowledge of the trueness of them?

Don't act in fear; fear is not the way to the promised land. It is what will lead you in circles and has led you in circles in the desert of man's abiding thus far.

Moses did not lead his people to the promised land, just as I did not during my time there. I have spoken of the reasons of that in my prior lesson and will not repeat it now, but I am crying out now that to find the promised land is to adopt and work the tenets of the American Constitution. People, it is the signpost; it is the neon sign saying, "Promised land this way!"

If you find yourself without knowledge of that written sign, then do not be a man or woman who compounds your ignorance by ignoring the sign. Do not wander in the desert with myopic vision. It is readily available to you. Find it, read it, dwell upon it, and see the brilliance.

Do you feel the glory within it? Can you not feel the true author? Lest a man think I am mad, which a few did in my day as a man, consider this: I am speaking now to you, and I am not a man. I am being given this power of speech and thought and the ability to record my words. What of that? If there is not a power that can be made available to me to tell of what I have seen, then how do you read my words?

I have been called forth to cry out. I have been given the privilege to cry out. I have been given one who can hear me to record my words. I have been given to know, and I share all with you, my brothers and sisters! Do not waste my gift or the gift that is being given to you with denial and fear-based rationalizations! Do not do as the men of Jesus's day when they saw and heard and turned their backs.

I am not Christ, but I have been given a gift to lead you as he had tried to do. Make no assumption that I am taking seriously those remarks made about me in my lifetime as being the little Messiah. I am not and will not take those things to heart. But I am a messenger, and I do take that seriously.

To sum up my conviction that I share with you today, I shall close by saying that my remarks in this are not meant to limit the use of man's mind only to the American way. To be sure, America has made her own disastrous mistakes. America is not the promised land. America is not the chosen of the Lord, but it is chosen to be a blueprint via ideology.

There is no greater way than to incorporate what works and what unites in the fight for world freedom. The tenets, as held in the writings of the founders of that country, are what I am talking about. Do not assume I am a biased man to America alone.

There are many great tenets in many other countries, but I have been shown the purpose for the founding of America.

I have seen the blueprint and the finished product. The American people do have reason to be proud of that writing that framed their country.

However, until it becomes a reality and not just a theory that founded the country, then their pride must be muted. Should you be a citizen of another country and do not know of their Constitution, then find the way to review it.

If you are a citizen living under that Constitution and taking for granted its freedom but have forgotten the entirety of those writings, then do your own review. This is the blueprint as was given to me as a sign post to the promised land—a land that does not inhabit a geographical location but a location in the hearts and minds of all men. Then surely shall we see the thousand years of peace! Amen, amen. Glory be to the Lord!

Ever striving and dreaming,

Martin

THE GIFT THAT GOT RETURNED

I have come to know the greater extent of man's folly. When you are here with no body and a form of expanded mind, you can quite easily plumb the depths of many things.

Due to the nature of my life lived there and my death through the fear and loathing of another, I was prompted to seek some knowledge of fear. I wanted to make sure I understood that process since I had discovered it as a hidden agenda within myself as explained in my first writing. What an interesting time I have had learning these things!

Did you know that man was once a species who knew no fear? That our first attempts at coming into flesh were done so with no knowledge of that concept?

Consider also a new baby. They do not know fear of anything. They might react to a loud noise or a bright light, but that is an autonomic nervous system reflex.

To know fear, as one does as they age, is not within the experience of a new baby. As I have said before, we teach much of those fears to our children, even if only by example.

When I discovered the truth that man had not always harbored fear in his mind, I began to mull that over. What changed? Who introduced fear? Why is it so prevalent in these latter days?

You can see where I would reflect upon that being, as I was, a victim of intense fear, can you not?

I have spent my days since leaving there make the study of fear my newest cause and have come forth now to share some of my knowledge with you.

Since each of these writings of mine are being given as individual treatises and yet also with an idea of making them cohesive enough to become a book, I will briefly cover some old ground to bring clarity and knowing to those who might have missed my earlier writings.

I am Martin Luther King Jr. In actuality, I am the spirit of that man who was known as such. In truth, I am not the man you knew by that name, but since it was my last incarnation, it does serve a purpose to express myself as that being. You can't be just a floating harp-playing angel and have people listen to you now, can you? No, my life there served a purpose; it is still celebrated, and this is why I define myself by that name. It is also because of that life as that man that I have gained a greater knowing of things related to fear and the effects of it upon men's minds.

I work delivering my treatises through the aid of one who can hear me. She is my typist and assistant. She does not generate the material, though she is good at correcting my sometimes incoherent ramblings.

We work as a team only in that editing process. She does not interject the veins of thought to these articles.

These are my ramblings, and she does well to hang with me through them. I commend her for her ability to type at such speed and yet know what needs to be changed in editing the mistakes I make grammatically. I could have used her when I wrote my speeches as Martin Luther!

I have discoursed upon the pocket of fear found within me upon my death. I have disclosed the hidden pockets of fear-generating systems that exist in the world. I have spoken of the effect of the American Constitution should it be given a chance at reality instead of staying a lofty ideal for the common man. I speak now on the things that have been lost by mankind.

Let us continue.

The loss of the ability to know no fear is a great one—perhaps one of the greatest setbacks mankind has ever known. With the loss of that golden gift, there has been a spinning out of control of the human species since that time.

MLK: TREATISES FROM MY LIFE

Sometimes the prevalence of fear gains great strides. Sometimes in history, there has been an abating of it in differing pockets of the world. But the slow and steady march of its roots have continued, and those things detested in the world today owe their entire genesis to that lost gift. Consider that if you will.

War? Caused by fear that one nation or country will dominate another, that one religion is correct, and another way of deity worship needs to be eradicated, and that sources of riches need to be controlled.

The war that besieges the world today is between fearful factions bent on religious dominance and control of the world's riches through the modern-day gold: oil. Can you deny my truth on this matter? Can you answer in dissent for that statement?

The abundance of those who turn to things like drink and drugs is rooted in a base of fear. The killing of each other is rooted in fear. The possession of material overabundance and the loss of personal commodities are rooted in fear. People, the decline of humanity is rooted in fear, and there is no need for such fear!

I have seen the wisdom of that statement and hope to alleviate you of these hidden roots. I wish to expose those roots and the needless and senseless effects of their taking hold any further in man's psyche.

Let me now make my case for the need to return to lack of fear.

It is my understanding now, having lost my earthly form, that God is benevolent. He is not a god of dire judgments. He is not a sorter of those who sin against him as I was once taught.

There is neither fiery punishments nor any turning away from God's graces. How gracious is it to turn away those who are in fear?

What Father would boot his children out of his home for becoming fearful of things that they do not understand? Get real with your own ideas of God's benevolence, children, and do not listen to those who would propagate fear-based teachings to gain control of your allegiance! They do so not because as a means to hold you to slavery, but because they have been taught to fear these very same things.

Fear is a reproducer, a sower of its own seeds if it is not choked out by love and wisdom. Use wisdom in understanding the love of God.

Fear not that God prefers any one segment over his other children. Fear not that if you are an uneducated man that you have less intrinsic value to God. Fear not that if you do not hoard, you will not have enough. Fear less that you are deserving of punishment for someone told you that you were wrong. Who are they, and where did their wisdom come from? Is it a form of that insidious fear creeping along their mental pathways? Do they know for a fact, as I do, what the true nature of heaven is about?

I speak now not from any pulpit with a man's understanding but from the platform of that place known as heaven and with the understanding of one having seen the glory. My voice is raised in volume now, not for the fear of the loss of heaven but with the praise of it.

I acclaim the truth that I did not know as I stood upon those pulpits and taught heaven to my followers. It is far more glorious that anything I understood as a man. There is no judgment, and there is only love.

Our example, Christ came to teach us not to fear. He showed no fear and obeisance to the religious men of his time. He spent many words upon, trying to show them their fear and the use of it to mislead others. He spat upon much of their notions.

His followers taught a more excellent way as well, but did we get it? Did I, as a minister, understand the truth of those teachings? I fear I did not and that you do not as well.

Where there is fear, there cannot exist true love. That is truly a golden rule our species have been missing.

In the lack of true love, can God be found?

It was one of Christ's followers who said that God is love. That is an absolute! It is the basis of all my knowledge gathered within this heaven where I now have my being.

MLK: TREATISES FROM MY LIFE

Since God is love and fear cannot reside with love, tell me, children, can God be found in those things that are spawned by fear? Is God in the wars you wage? Does God truly exist in a fearful nation, a fearful town, or a fearful home? Does God sanction one who hoards and does not share due to fear of lack?

I am fairly certain you know the answers to those questions if you *think* for yourselves. That is my purpose: *Think*, children. Do not let fear do your thinking for you!

The gift of knowing no fear is a gift that may be returned to men. It may take a while for it to arrive, but it is a guaranteed delivery if you order it. It will be sent by express courier if you but purchase it. You do not even have to wait at home for its arrival. It will find you no matter where you are.

There will be no fancy wrappings. It will not come with a gift tag; you will know who sent it. It will not have bells and whistles, but it will be of highest quality. It will not suffer damage in its travels to you. I beseech you all to pick up your minds and hearts and order it at once.

And remember, this is not a limited time offer. It will be available always. It has no "first come, first served" warning. There is a stockpile of it sufficient for all. No need to wait, no need to push, and shove in line for it.

I have seen the stockpile. I have asked for and been given my own gift. Why do without that gift of lack of fear when it is but a decision away?

I close now and wish you all the grace I have witnessed. I have judged myself and yet felt no judgment through love. There *is* a package here with *your* name upon it. Have no fear of that!

Martin Luther King, a Spirit of Jubilation and Exultation

There Is a Sun Arising in Canaan

The will of the Israelites to follow the leader Moses to the promised land was inspired by belief.

Belief is the fuel for many great marches. It is the fuel for many great changes. It is the fuel for what is coming to your world and the fulfillment of the finding of the promised land within every home.

When Moses set forth out across that barren desert for a land he had not yet seen, he had faith. Those who followed him into that wasteland had faith. When I set forth upon my marches for freedom, I had faith. Those who followed my associates and I had faith.

Faith is the key word here if you have not yet seen that coming. Faith is what makes the formation of any column of marchers a reality. Faith is what is needed today.

But faith in what? Where is the great ideal that will inspire faith for those who must line up in the marches? Where are the lines forming? Who is leading? Where is the faith coming from?

Yes, those are pertinent questions. They are the questions that need to be asked. But let me say, there are no questions being asked loudly enough and with enough minds for your world to form answers. Most sit idly by and let the world continue as it has.

Many do not care enough to get out of their easy chairs and look about to see if lines are forming for marches to the promised land. Many think because they have easy chairs and televisions and homes and cars that they are living in the promised land. What

MLK: TREATISES FROM MY LIFE

fools will suffer when their backsides are not marked with whip-lashes and bent with manual labor!

Do those of you sitting in easy chairs with the televisions entrancing you really think you are living the life that would be described as promised? Do you think that because you have no needs of physical sustenance that you have arrived in the land of milk and honey? What of your brothers and sisters who have no milk or honey? Do you think they are as fat and contented as you are? Can your world be described as a promised land if there are people sleeping in boxes and under bridges, if children are left to fend for themselves and go to sleep hungry? What of the spiritual qualities to this land that you abide in? Does it measure up as equally in stature to your ideals of physical comfort? How can you sit in the chairs and eat the food when you are a spiritually starv-ing people? If there was a fatness to your spiritual life as there is to your physical life, then neither a man nor a woman nor a child would be downcast and forgotten. That is the measure of a full spiritual world.

I know, who am I to come back from the dead and lay this upon you? Who am I, a former preacher and man of some renown, to be laying this rap at your feet? Who am I to be so arrogant as to challenge your world and its systems?

Hate me if you will, but it is my goal to make you mad; mad at me, mad at my audacity, mad at the prod to your consciousness.

I come to make you think! I come to make you look about you and really *see* the state of affairs you reside in. I come as one who led folks to a version of the promised land, and as I have said, I led them with a righteous idea in my head but fear in my heart.

That is a truth. But I want now to lead you all to a clear understanding what the complacency of your world is costing you in terms of spiritual bounty.

I judge you not, but as I have also said, it is not I or another who will judge you when sit where I am now. It is you who will judge, and I seek only to save you some of the torments that I have had to endure over my own judgments pronounced upon myself. *If* you do not wake now, you will not rest in peace later! I have never before pronounced a truer statement from any pulpit!

As you read my words, perhaps from that very same blasphemed easy chair, I have hoped you will see what I am saying. It is not about what you have but what you are willing to give. It is not about what you eat but about what you share. It is not about the size of your bank account but the size of your heart and the willingness to have others share in your bounty.

These are the things that count toward spiritual richness and fatness of soul. It is about the use of your life to enrich the world, not just your family. It is about the finding of the man who lives in the promised land in his mind and leads others there as well. It is about having faith that each step you make will take the world toward that land of milk and honey.

Speaking of faith, as you know I have done in my earthly life and as I am now doing, there is not one life that exists that is not arisen from faith. Read that again, children. There is not one life that is not arisen from faith. Now what is the crazy dead man talking about? I can hear the thoughts as you read this. I understand those thoughts, but it does not erase the truth of that statement. There is not one life that is not arisen from faith.

Faith in the unseen, faith in things not yet beheld—that is what this crazy man is talking about.

These are the hallmarks of belief. Could any life bloom if we do not hold hope that tomorrow would come? Would we strive so hard for ourselves and our children if we did not have faith that it would serve us tomorrow? Would any life exist if our parents had not had faith that to reproduce would produce a hope for a better tomorrow? Yes, yes, I know, some are produced without thought to tomorrow, but you get what I am saying.

There must be faith for life to be worth living. It is a remarkable facet of the human nature to have faith in things not readily beheld, and that is why the human race continues to reproduce, strive, grow, and pioneer. Faith is the fuel.

Now to round out my flow of thought here, what would be the value to human life if faith did not exist? What would be the

MLK: TREATISES FROM MY LIFE

fuel if faith was taken away? What about if faith was misdirected or used in a way to fuel those things not good for the human race? Do you see where this is going? Can you see now why I say that faith is the fuel? And what kind of fuel are you generating for the human rocket ship? Is it sufficient to get you to where you want to go? Is it a fuel that will lift the ship to the heavens or only propel it into a never-ending orbit around the same old view of Earth? Has it become so diluted that it is going to be a crash and burn situation?

Speaking of rocket ships, I had the marvel of seeing mankind head out to space in my life there. I saw the launches then as a hope that we would tame new frontiers.

That mankind would someday become master of a new horizon. The culmination of that dream of heading out to space was the by-product of faith that we could do so.

I know that man ultimately did reach the heavens literally after my death, and that has great bearing on my sermon today. Without that faith that mankind could get men to the moon, would you have gone? Would you have tried and succeeded as you have?

There is great parallel here to what I am saying to you: Without the fuel of faith, there would have been no rocket ships. Without faith, there would not have been one man who would have entered the chambers of those ships to risk life to try. Without faith, not a soul would know what you do about the physical heavens that has been gleaned by having the faith that launched those rockets. Without faith that you can make a difference, you won't launch the rockets of attempt and then bask in the marvel of knowing that you did.

I would not leave you here without hope. I would not close my sermon to you without a tie-in to my topic.

In the metaphorical land of Canaan, there was a sun of great strength arising. It was the sun of hope, and it was the glow of combined efforts given rise from faith.

You must have faith in those things not yet seen upon your world. You must have faith that each man and woman can and will make a difference that will move the entirety of the world toward a new promised land. You must have faith that if you leave those easy chairs and offer the world a bit of your time and resources that others will follow your lead.

Faith that as one man begins the march toward Canaan, that others will join the line, and the march grows. Faith that as each person steps but one step closer that the entire line behind him will do so as well. If there is not faith that the land may be reached someday, then the entire line behind you is lost.

Had the man Moses not had faith, the Israelites would have been lost to the plight in Egypt. From his faith grew the faith of others.

From *your* faith grows the faith of others. Be like Moses and lead. Be an Israelite and follow the man in front of you. Rest not for the land of Canaan is glowing mightily in front of you!

It is there, it is real, and it has been seen in the minds of many men. It is the life that is deserved by everyone, not the selected few.

Your steps today, tomorrow, and every day after will but bring you that much closer.

The way to ease and comfort in your soul does not come from that downy easy chair or that undulating television screen. It comes from marching—marching for a new life and a new land where your children will partake of a richness that has nothing to do with wealth.

It is a long trail, children. Have no doubt. There will be great expanses of barren wasteland. There will be feelings of lack and confusion. But did those things not make the Israelites rejoice even more when the land had been reached? Do have faith that your rejoicing, whether it be of that world or of this one, will be every bit as sweet and that the rewards just as well-deserved as those found by the ones who let their faith guide them to follow their Moses.

One who walks with you,

Martin

THE WAYS AND MEANS
TO SALVATION

Now is the time when I must close my sermons to your world. Not for eternity but rather through the use of this woman who has served me well in getting my thoughts to paper.

She has been a mighty aid and a joy to work with, but it is for both our benefit that we find ourselves coming to the conclusion of our time together.

I have given her a nod for aiding me, and I wish to convey once again that the use of her is only to lay words to paper.

The ideas and the tones found within this body of work are my own. She is a good editor but not the genesis of these treatises. This is to be made abundantly clear, for I wish no repercussions to her for my work and do not wish for her to take credit, be it in infamy or fame, for these words. I stand alone in this except for the use of her hands and mind to convey these words to you.

I once preached a means to salvation. I once worked up sweats and nerves, trying to get my flock to follow the path to salvation.

Many of the things I spoke of were indeed heartfelt. I would not have been one who would repeat those things I did not believe in.

I often spoke of the ways of the Lord as I understood it and had been given to understand it, and of that, I am free to say that I felt no remorse. I was a man on fire, trying to find my own salvation and the leading of others to it.

As pure as my heart was then with the convictions of my beliefs, I must say that I have been shown a more excellent way.

Those things that I spoke of and believed in then were but the understanding of a babe who had not grown in the fullest of knowledge. Perhaps even now I am but a babe in the true fullest of knowledge, but what I wish to share today is what I have come to know and believe since having left my earthly pulpits. Today I stand to correct a few of my former statements.

I was fired up with the idea that should I, or others, live in such and such a way, then glory and salvation would be ours. But I have come to know that even those who do not live in such ways also share in life eternal.

All share the glory of eternal life. This is fact. It is something I now know and wish to share. Do others deserve it that do not follow the ways of the Lord as I was once told? Yes. Does there exist a judgment for things done in man's time on earth? Yes, but is it a sorting of those who would perish from the memory of the Lord and be banned to places of torment? No.

There is no such arrangement here. There is no turning away from the Lord's attention. There is no judgment, but that which is passed upon oneself as I have said before several times in these writings. There is no end to life eternal, and there is no scale that determines who perishes and who resides forever in the Lord's care.

I use here some of the phrases of my former ministry. I use here the phrases of the ministries being taught in many lands and many cultures. But the truth of the matter is that the language of these statements are confining. How do you use words to convey the vastness of eternity, the vastness of the love that is deity?

None exists that is not in the care of love. None exists that is deserving of eternal destruction. Yes, the body may be changed as clothes are changed when traveling from one place to another. The personality may alter as it does even over an earthly lifetime. But the essence, the essence of who I was before I became Martin Luther King and of who I am now that I am not any longer that mere man, continues. It is the eternal aspect of us all, and it is ever in the care of love.

MLK: TREATISES FROM MY LIFE

My life as a man does not define me. My works as that man should not define all of who I am.

I utilize that aspect of who I am to reach your world, for I had made a notable life there through the guidance of love. But I am and ever will be more than just the life of Martin Luther King Jr. I could not have done the things I did had I known, fully known, all of who I was at that time. It would have altered my perception of things in the world, and that would have altered my actions. But the fact that I achieved what I did came through the promptings of love, and I played my role as I was intended.

It was a role of freedom seeker, and I now seek freedom for men's minds.

Where I sought the freedom of men's minds from prejudice and hate, do I not still seek the freedom of men's minds from fear and misinformation, the basis of those things I fought against while there? Had I known that I would not ever find myself cast off from God's graces, would I have tried so hard to lead men to the glory of salvation? Would I have found the conviction in me to fight the fight that I did?

I must say that perhaps not, but do not misunderstand me here. I would have known that I would always find the face of God and that others would do the same. I would have known that the things I fought against were but transitory in the real vastness of eternity. But that does not mean that I would not have fought to make other men see and other men to know what I knew. I would have fought, but it would have been more equal to the fight I now wage in freeing men not from the shackles of other men's fear and hate, but from their own.

When one assumes that this life being led is the only life, then there is great room for things, such as greed, dissention, and hate. When one fights to gain a salvation that they are being told only comes to their brand of belief, there is even more room for hate and fear. When people are led to believe that justice is meted out by some vengeful force, then how great their fear grows!

However, when one knows that those whom you see as infidels also will deserve a plot of land in eternity and will become your neighbors there, where is the room for greed and fear? How does it behoove you to fight with those you will see over and over again in the cycles of life? What if men knew that all were loved equally and that what role you play now will be reversed in the days to come? Does this not add a new dimension to the ways and means to salvation?

I risk the reputation of my own former life, my former beliefs, and my former actions to come forth now and tell you the truth of things as I have determined them. I risk the reputation of the one who does nothing but type my words, though this should not be.

But I do so because I still seek to freemen, not men of color, men of poverty, or even men of certain religious beliefs. I seek to free all men and women as well, mind you, of the choking and killing influence of wrong beliefs.

To believe that you must earn eternal life and that others may not possess, it is a wrong belief. To believe that one way, one nation, one religion, any one anything is the only way to the Lord's graces is wrong. This is very, very wrong. To hold another as less than you because they are not Catholic or white or tall or smart or whatever your belief should be is wrong.

The face of deity knows none of these things as *less than*. The face of deity, should you call that deity God or Allah or Bubba is not concerned with the transitory things of this world.

There is no judgment from deity. That is a man-made conception that is in error.

But this error is the foundations of the many things that others used to judge one another. It is the basis of separation and segregation of the brotherhood of mankind. It is the metaphorical serpent in the Garden of Eden!

Think now of the strife in your world. Is it not because of judgment? Is it not because someone thinks another's way of being is wrong? What about the wars being waged now because one group feels another is not correct in their beliefs about deity? What about the man who robs another because he feels the other has more than he does? Is that a form of judgment that someone else does not deserve what labor and toil has brought to him? If each of you, in your earlier spoken of easy chair, were consumed with judging your own beliefs, actions, and control of resources, then where would be the time to judge your neighbor? *Do* you see the rafter in your own eye? Who are you judging and why? Let thy neighbor alone see first to your own house and the rooms within it. Sweep only your own home, for if your home is not clean, then can there be judgment of another?

When the world releases the error of thinking that any one person despite their beliefs, their color, their actions, or their worth in earthy value is less than in the eyes of deity, then shall they know the peace of this world. There is no acrimony in this world for there is no basis of judgment of another, only of self. If self is found lacking, then choices are made about correction of those things. But judgment of another is not found here, either by self or deity. It is not known and it is not a fact of this world.

Let that world understand what it is I try to do. I try and correct even my own assumptions of that time as the man Martin. I try and ignite the understanding that judgment and the false belief in judgment of deity are the root of all evil in that world. It is not, as the old saying goes, money but rather judging one through the means of money, color, and beliefs in deity.

Can you change the world through a change of beliefs? Oh, how mighty that indeed would be! How great the freedom when the beliefs change!

But you can only change your own beliefs. To judge another for the beliefs they hold is not the thing, you see.

You must change the world by your own action and leave the action of others for their own judgment. But if all could know of the freedom of releasing judgment, then soon the shift would become widespread.

As each man decides the value of what I and others say from this world, then changes their mode of beliefs and therefore judgments, the world would correct much of the things not conducive to peace.

ROSE CAMPBELL

Peace is never found in judgment. It is found when that love that is deity is expressed in lack of judgment. This is the ways and means of salvation to your world.

Martin

CONCLUSION

There you have it. What Martin, or more precisely the spirit that had been Martin Luther King Jr., felt compelled to say.

I can honestly say that I had not considered most of what he spoke of. As I said, I knew very little of the man until his contact Sent me into research mode. However, I found that as I took dictation and these tenets and wisdoms were made known to me that I found myself agreeing with most of it.

It is not truly for me to agree or not agree on what I received; it is my job to record and pass forward. It does help though if I can relate to it, and it opens new channels (pun intended!) of understanding within me. I hope you find the same thing for yourself.

To conclude this book, I am using a quote that I came to love as a child. It is simple and direct and it says it all in vast many ways: "That's all, folks!"

CPSIA information can be obtained
at www.ICGtesting.com
Printed in the USA
BVHW081200090522
636525BV00020B/137